A MANUAL
OF
ENGLISH METERS

Joseph Malof , 1934 -

Indiana University Press
Bloomington, London

PE
1505
.M3
1970

Library of Congress catalog card number: 70–98979

SBN: 253-33674-0

Published in Canada by Fitzhenry & Whiteside Limited, Don Mills, Ontario.

Manufactured in the United States of America.

For
John Crowe Ransom

CONTENTS

Contents

Contents

PREFACE

This book is not an argument in support of some theory. It is a repository of information. It provides principles, mechanisms, and vocabulary for reading and talking about poetic meters.

No one pretends that putting labels on certain poetic features is an end in itself. But it can be very useful to have a vocabulary with which to support whatever we do want to say about the technical dimensions of a poem. This book undertakes the limited task of making available as many of the metrical concepts and terminologies as the teacher, student, scholar, poet, and general reader are likely to want in writing, reading, and discussing poetry.

This is, therefore, a kind of reference book, containing more information about the tools and techniques of scansion than is, perhaps, available elsewhere. This book also serves as an introduction to meters. Except for the final chapter, the focus is frankly technical; I have not attempted to stimulate an appreciation of poetry in general, to interpret the esthetic effects of metrical phenomena, or to plumb the linguistic realities of poetic recitation. Such things will continue to be done in other books and articles. The aim here has been to give the reader some equipment with which to pursue those more ambitious discussions and, more importantly, to give him the means to respond more fully to the metrical dimension of poetry.

The referential function of this book is implemented further by the appendixes, which provide in compressed form information on such auxiliary matters as stanzas, rhymes, a glossary giving terms not used in the main text (or giving definitions that vary from the ones adopted in the text), and recommended readings. Stanzas and rhymes are not always thought to fall within the domain of metrical analysis, but their involvement with meter in actual poems is often a very close one: stanzas are often effective "packages" of metrical units, and rhymes often serve as boundaries for metrical sequences. Since, however, they cannot be covered fully here, the basic information about them is given in the appendixes, in order that this volume may be more useful as a handbook. Titles of poems and names of poets are relegated to another appendix so that the main body of the text can depict metrical structures in undisturbed focus. Another appendix summarizes the essentials of common poetic forms and symbols of scansion, to facilitate quick reference.

If, on one level, this book is a manual of metrical analysis, and on another level, an introduction to poetic meters, on a third level it represents the fruition of a theory of metrical scansion. Every metrist to some degree invents his own system of metric, building upon the concepts available to him and upon his own ideas of organization and utility. Every system of metrics is the result of one person's decisions on where and how to draw from earlier traditions, what to reject as unhelpful, where to modify existing definitions, and where to initiate new ones. The emphasis of this book, however, is not on the assumptions or theories behind metrical scansion but on the system of scansion itself. Instead of arguing for a theory, it applies theory: it presents the structure completed, with the theoretical scaffolding removed.

In order to forestall one major point of possible confusion, I should like to emphasize that this book is not a summary of the historical development of metrical terms. The aim here is to draw on the best of what is available, in whole or in part. Some terms, for example, are used here as complementary to each other although they originated in systems that contradicted one another; other terms have been redefined for more immediate usefulness. Usefulness is the main criterion: meter, after all, is an invented language for "measuring" certain linguistic elements, and the methods of measurement will depend on the needs of the measurer.

I have freely adopted from the works of others, and sometimes adapted, terms and concepts both of theory and of mechanics, under the assumption that by their nature they belong to the public domain. I have also made bold to plunder the books of other metrists for illustrations of metrical forms. These illustrations are so many and varied that accurate acknowledgment of the sources, after determining who first found the line or poem, would be impractical and at this late stage downright impossible. For my own contribution, I offer a few dozen long-hunted lines and some new technical terms and concepts.

Many of the symbols of scansion used here are gleaned from other systems, and sometimes adapted. I have found them, particularly the ones used in foot-scansion, to be serviceable in practice, clear, simple, flexible, and capable of duplication on the typewriter. The typewriter also is argument for scanning below the line, which keeps the words of the poem in view, is less confusing when the eye becomes accustomed to it, and maintains the proper subordination of meter to poem. However, some scansions are given above the line and a number of symbols are used interchangeably, in order to illustrate the different techniques available for different needs.

My indebtedness to the works of numerous metrists accumulates with every page. But my greatest debt is to my wife, Dannie, whose incisive readings of the manuscript always resulted in suggestions that were helpful and enlightening. I am also particularly thankful to Martha Wailes for her help in improving and preparing the manuscript.

Acknowledgments

W. H. Auden, "Stop All the Clocks," "As I Walked Out," and "O Where Are You Going" from *Collected Shorter Poems 1927–1957*. By permission of Random House, Inc. Published in Great Britain by Faber and Faber Ltd.

E. E. Cummings, "i am so glad and very," "except in your," "anyone lived in a pretty how town," "my father moved through dooms of love," and "when god decided to invent" from *Poems 1923–1954*. By permission of Harcourt, Brace & World, Inc. and MacGibbon & Kee Ltd. "except in your" copyright, 1944, by E. E. Cummings. Reprinted from his volume *Poems 1923–1954* by permission of Harcourt, Brace & World, Inc.

T. S. Eliot, "Whispers of Immortality," "Sweeney Among the Nightingales," "East Coker," "The Love Song of J. Alfred Prufrock," "Burnt Norton," "The Dry Salvages," and "The Waste Land" from *Collected Poems 1909–1962*; "The Cocktail Party" from *Collected Plays*. By permission of Faber & Faber Ltd. and Harcourt, Brace & World, Inc. From "The Dry Salvages" in *Four Quartets*, copyright, 1943, by T. S. Eliot. Reprinted by permission of Harcourt, Brace & World, Inc. From "The Waste Land" in *Collected Poems 1909–1962* by T. S. Eliot, copyright, 1936, by Harcourt, Brace & World, Inc.; copyright ©, 1963, 1964, by T. S. Eliot. Reprinted by permission of the publisher. From *The Cocktail Party*, copyright, 1950, by T. S. Eliot. Reprinted by permission of Harcourt, Brace & World, Inc.

Gerard Manley Hopkins, "I wake and feel," "The Wreck of the *Deutschland*," "Heaven-Haven," and "God's Grandeur" from *Poems*, edited by Robert Bridges. By permission of Oxford University Press, Inc.

Vachel Lindsay, "The Congo" from *Collected Poems*. By permission of The Macmillan Company.

Amy Lowell, "Patterns" from *The Complete Poetical Works of Amy Lowell*. By permission of Houghton Mifflin Company.

Marianne Moore, "He 'Digesteth Harde Yron'" and "To a Snail" from *Collected Poems*. By permission of The Macmillan Company, The Macmillan Company of Canada Ltd., and Faber and Faber Ltd.

John Crowe Ransom, "Bells for John Whiteside's Daughter," "Dead Boy," "Janet Waking," and "Captain Carpenter" from *Poems and Essays*. By permission of Alfred A. Knopf, Inc.

Wallace Stevens, "Peter Quince at the Clavier," "The Red Fern," "The Idea of Order at Key West," and "The Pleasures of Merely Circulating" from *Poems*. By permission of Alfred A. Knopf, Inc.

Richard Wilbur, "Junk" from *Advice to a Prophet* and "Museum Piece" from *Poems 1943–1956*. By permission of Faber & Faber Ltd. and Harcourt, Brace & World, Inc.

W. B. Yeats, "News For the Delphic Oracle," "September 1913," "Lapis Lazuli," "The Circus Animal's Desertion," and "Easter 1916" from *Collected Poems*. By permission of The Macmillan Company.

A MANUAL OF ENGLISH METERS

CHAPTER I
BASIC TERMS AND SYMBOLS

Language used in ordinary prose has a rhythm, but this **prose rhythm** does not follow any preset pattern. Even when it leaves some kind of rhythmic pattern in its wake as it flows along, it is not formally organized and is not predictable to a significant degree.

When language passes into poetry it is no longer used for simple communication. Its rhythms, no longer mere decorations for the meanings, are put on exhibition. And partly through the help of the rhythms, poetic language itself becomes a stylization of prose language. It is in this sense an artificial language.

So the rhythms of poetry, compared with prose rhythms, are stylized and artificial; they fall into patterns that are more repetitive and predictable. That is, poetic rhythms appear to be organized. They begin to call attention to themselves, and we begin to be interested in their organization. We then develop a vocabulary for talking about the patterns they take.

Our sense of rhythm in language is dependent on many linguistic features: the beat, emphasis, or stress of the syllables; their length, pitch, environment, and so forth. Traditional meter in English takes as its basic building block the first of these elements, **stress.** Stress is one of those linguistic activities that no one has completely defined but that almost everyone can recognize. For our purposes we will simply define it as a syllable that appears *more* emphatic or important than its neighbor, one that gives rhythmic "beat" to the line of poetry. By organizing the frequency and position of stressed syllables into patterns, we construct **metrical rhythms.**

1

This does not mean, by the way, that poetic meter must always be a matter of arranging stresses. A "meter" is after all merely a tool of measurement, like a yardstick, and any prominent feature of a language can be used as the recurring "marker." Some languages are sensitive to syllabic length, and they construct their "quantitative" meters by distinguishing between long and short syllables; others go according to syllabic pitch, thus making "isotonic" verse; and others go simply according to the total number of syllables in the line, making "syllabic" verse. But English meters generally (with the syllabic verse discussed in Chapter V the notable exception) are *accentual*, built on a recurrence of *stressed* syllables.

METER AND RHYTHM

In the freer varieties of accentual verse, meter is determined simply by counting the number of stresses in the line of poetry, ignoring the relatively unemphatic or unstressed syllables, which we will call **slacks**. Over the past centuries, however, the most popular system has been more demanding and has been concerned with both stresses and slacks, their number, ratio, and position in the line. In this system (called foot-verse in Chapter II), the structure is formed by repeating a basic rhythmical unit of stressed and slack syllables. Several such units are possible: we can have a slack followed by a stress (let us symbolize this as x —), the reverse (— x), two slacks followed by a stress (xx —), the reverse of that (— xx), and so forth. When a certain unit recurs frequently or regularly (as in the pattern xx —|xx —|xx —|xx . . .), we say that the *rhythms* have been regularized into a *meter*.

The general meter of a poem and the actual rhythms of specific lines in that poem are not always identical. Few poems consist of rhythmic units (say x —) that are repeated without any variation. Yet in many poems the rhythms will fall into some kind of *over-all* pattern, and it is the basic characteristic of that pattern that we call the meter. If, for example, the |x —| unit predominates throughout a poem, the meter of that poem is probably based on it. We cannot predict for certain that any given cluster of syllables will fall perfectly into the metrical design; nevertheless, designs do emerge from the varying rhythms, and some of them, through long tradition, have taken root and become standardized metrical conventions. So *the meter is a simplification and generalization about what the rhythms tend to do.*

Yet while meter is the design formed *by* the rhythms, as soon as it takes firm shape in our minds it becomes also a fixed authority, a conservative estimate of rhythmic tendencies, a standard *against* which the freer, more liberal rhythms seem to move. It is as though the rhythms in a poem elect a meter to represent them in the poetic structure, only to turn around and assert themselves against its authority. A meter, then, grows out of the natural linguistic rhythms of the words but is also in a continual state of tension with them.

This interplay between rhythm and meter is important, because once we discover the metrical plan of a poem, we try to follow it even to the point of altering, within reasonable limits, our rhythmic reading of specific lines. For example, a normal "prose" reading of this well-known line would be:

Péas pórridge in the pót

but when we follow the metrical "beat" we are accustomed to, we tend to alter the pronunciation to:

Péas pórridge ín the pót

giving a full stress to the rhythmically insignificant word "in."

The best device for recording the tension between meter and rhythm is **scansion**. Scansion is not a mere diagram of the meter, repeating the basic unit over and over. Neither is it a transcription of the prose rhythms, giving all the subtleties and varieties of pronunciation. It is a combination, a system of notation that attempts, *as far as usefully possible*, to indicate the main characteristics of the meter and the main deviations of the rhythm from the metrical pattern. It compromises between simplicity and complexity, since an overly simple system would not give enough detailed information about rhythmical activities, and an overly detailed one would not convey a sense of the general metrical design or set of laws. In scansion we learn the rhythmical rules, and we also get some idea of how, and where, and how much the poet breaks them.

Here are some of the basic terms, symbols, and concepts of scansion. Most of them will be given fuller illustration and development in appropriate later chapters.

SYMBOLS

Most systems of scansion require a minimum of three symbols, to represent:

    —   a syllable counting metrically as stress

    x   a syllable counting metrically as slack

    | a division marker or bar between repeated units, groups, or clusters of syllables.

For example, in

> Taffy was a Welshman
> — x — x —   x

we examine the rhythmical pattern to decide how the stresses and slacks can be most clearly and economically grouped so as to show a simple repeated unit of measurement. One possibility in this case is:

> — x|— x|— x

which records the rhythmical organization as consisting of a unit of one stress plus one slack, repeated three times. Any such unit clearly repeated throughout the line can be taken as a standard of measurement and is commonly called a **foot**.

The line we have just scanned accordingly has three feet. Here is a line with four feet of the opposite pattern:

Upon a golden horse he sat.
x − |x −| x   − | x −

The pattern of a poem can easily become more complicated:

O where ha you been, Lord Randal, my son?
x   −   x x   −   x   − x   x −

We may divide this line in several ways:

x|− xx|− x|− xx|−   (− xx twice)

or   x −|xx −|x −|xx −   (x − twice and xx − twice)

or   x − x|x − x|− x|x −   (x − x twice)

Or we may decide that none of the groupings is dominant enough to make all this notation and foot division worthwhile. So we may choose to mark only the stresses and ignore the slack syllables:

− − − −

DEGREES OF STRESS

It is useful to have another symbol for the times when we are interested only in the stresses, or when the slacks do not appear regularly enough to form a consistent pattern. It is also useful to have some way of distinguishing between the strongest or **primary stresses** and the not-quite-so-strong or **secondary stresses** (remembering that we are not now dealing with slacks at all). So another way of scanning the line might be:

O whére ha you béen, Lord Rándal, my són?

where the double accent records the primary stress and the single accent the secondary stress. If we do not want to distinguish between primaries and secondaries, or if we are not able to, we can simplify the notation:

And whére ha you béen, my hándsome young mán?

Sometimes we are in doubt as to how a syllable ought to be scanned. In such cases we must remind ourselves of the difference between the prose rhythms of the language and the metrical pattern built out of those rhythms. When in doubt, we can begin by marking the prose rhythm, or leaving question marks, and then comparing the data with the metrical pattern that seems to emerge elsewhere in the poem. Suppose we arrive at the line:

And leaves the world to darkness and to me.
x   —   x —   x — x x x —

Having given it the prose scansion, we then examine the metrical **context**, the other lines in the same poem. We find that this line carries only four stresses while the others carry five:

		stresses
1	The Curfew tolls the knell of parting day, x — x — x — x — x —	5
2	The lowing herd wind slowly o'er the lea, x — x — x — x — x —	5
3	The plowman homeward plods his weary way, x — x — x — x — x —	5
4	And leaves the world to darkness and to me. x — x — ⸝x — x x x —	4?

Suspecting now that line 4 ought also to have five stresses, we look in it for a slack syllable that will allow itself to be **promoted** to the metrical rank of stress, carrying more emphasis than ordinarily, yet not so much as to distort the pronunciation beyond reasonable limits (as would happen if we promoted "the"). The syllable we want should be a **medial** stress, somewhere between the general stress level and the general slack level. In looking for it, we need to be aware of several *degrees* of emphasis that we give syllables when normally speaking, so let us make a short digression.

For the purposes of scansion we can more or less arbitrarily set up four general levels of prose-rhythm stress: *primary, secondary, tertiary,* and *weak.* Our system of English meter, however, constructs patterns by using only two elements: *stress* and *slack.* This means that we must transcribe our four-level pattern of the rhythm into the two-level (or binary) pattern of the meter. In doing so, we can regard *primaries* as metrical stresses, and *weaks* as slacks. The ones in the two middle levels (the medials) could go either way, although *secondaries* would as a rule become stresses while *tertiaries* would become slacks. (If a tertiary syllable does in fact have to be promoted to metrical stress, it is called **ictus**). Here is a table giving the four rhythmical levels of stress and their two-level reduction in meter:

degree of stress	*name*	*symbol*	*metrical rank*	*quality*
1	primary	—	stress	always —
2	secondary	ˆ	medial	ordinarily — but possibly x by demotion
3	tertiary	ˆ		ordinarily x but possibly — by promotion (ictus)
4	weak	x	slack	always x

In the scansion, then, medials do not remain such: they are finally put into one class or the other of our binary system. So to say that a syllable is medial is to say merely that it has not yet been *determined.* We can mark these undetermined syllables with question marks, but a more convenient symbol is the circumflex, ˆ, which allows us to place beneath it later

the mark that shows whether it has been determined as stress
($\hat{-}$) or as slack ($\hat{x}$).

How do we find a syllable that, marked slack in our scansion of the prose rhythm, is really a medial that can be promoted to stress? We use all the clues we have. We listen more carefully to the rhythm of the line. We also use external information. We know, for example, that, on the rhythmic level of English poetry, a congregating of three stresses (– – –) or three slacks (x x x) is usually suspicious. We found such a pattern near the end of our problem line:

And leaves the world to darkness and to me.
                          x   x   x

But which of these three slacks ought we to promote? Rule of thumb: with three consecutive slacks, try first to promote the middle one. We can do so in this case without creating unreasonable distortion in the pronunciation:

And leaves the world to darkness and to me.
x   –   x   – x –   x $\overset{-}{\underset{\uparrow}{}}$ x –

This modification does not seem to be unreasonable. How does the line as now scanned compare with the other lines in the stanza? Not only does it supply the missing fifth stress; it also brings the ten syllables of the line into a perfect stress sequence of two-syllable units, |x –|x –|x –|x –|x –|, which is exactly the sequence in the other lines. So, by promoting the medial syllable "and," we have finally rendered a metrical scansion of the line. We may now drop the circumflex for the sake of simplicity:

And leaves the world to darkness and to me.
x   – |x   – |x – | x   – | x –

Much of the time, hearkening to the metrical patterns, we determine medials automatically and make no special record of it. Readers vary in sensitivity to promotions or the need to record them. In the stanza above, some will see nothing unordinary in line two while others will want to record the **demotion** at the fifth syllable:

> The lowing herd wind slowly o'er the lea
> x — | x   — | x̂   — | x — | x —

Likewise there seemed to be no need to record the promotion in "Taffy was a Welshman."

In sum, *promotion* is the process of scanning a tertiary stress as a metrical *stress*. *Demotion* is the process of scanning a secondary stress as a metrical *slack*. In the following passage, note the promotions and demotions and the places where the basic unit (here x —) must be varied to avoid an unreasonably distorted pronunciation:

> Poor soul, the center of my sinful earth,
> x̂   — | x   — |x -̂ | x — |x   —

> Lord of these rebel pow'rs that thee array,
> x̂ -̂ | x   — |x   — | x   — |x —
> or   — x |

> Why dost thou pine within and suffer dearth,
> x̂ -̂ | x   — | x — | x   — |x   —
> or   — x |

> Painting thy outward walls so costly gay?
> — x | x — | x   — | x — |x   —

> Why so large cost, having so short a lease,
> x̂ -̂ |x̂   — | — x | x   — | x —
> or   — x |—   x |

> Dost thou upon thy fading mansion spend?
> x   — | x — | x — |x   — |x   —

Shall worms, inheritors of this excess,
x   – |x   –|x̂ |x   –|x –

Eat up thy charge? Is this thy body's end?
      x̂ – | x   – | x –| x – |x –
or   – x |

CESURA

In English poetry, most lines of more than three stresses tend to *break* into **sections**, usually two. Such breaks mark a division in meaning, in the logical grouping of ideas. Although a break often contributes to metrical effects, it is not determined by the meter. It is called the **cesura** and is symbolized by two vertical lines: ‖ .

One way of learning to "see" a cesura is to ask: "If I had to break this line into two main pieces of meaning, where would be the most logical place to do it?" Since the cesura is involved with the meaning of the words, it is signaled in the syntax and therefore often by the punctuation:

O whére ha you béen, Lord Rándal, my són?
‖

And whére ha you béen, my hándsome young mán?
‖

In this case the cesura divides the lines perfectly in half, breaking four stresses into two groups of two.

In lines containing an odd number of stresses, the cesura cannot of course fall at the center, but it usually comes close to it. In a line containing five stresses, for example, the cesura will often be found either between the second and third stresses or between the third and fourth:

But where's the man, who counsel can bestow,
1   2 ‖   3   4   5

Still pleas'd to teach, and yet not proud to know?
1   2 ‖   3   4   5

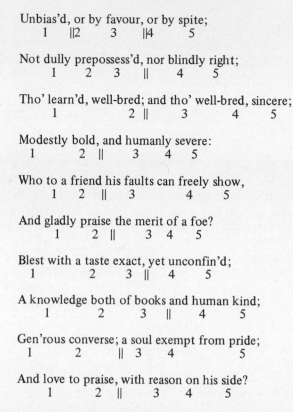

Unbias'd, or by favour, or by spite;
1 ||2   3 ||4   5

Not dully prepossess'd, nor blindly right;
    1   2   3 || 4   5

Tho' learn'd, well-bred; and tho' well-bred, sincere;
    1   2 || 3   4   5

Modestly bold, and humanly severe:
    1   2 || 3   4   5

Who to a friend his faults can freely show,
    1   2 || 3   4   5

And gladly praise the merit of a foe?
    1   2 || 3   4   5

Blest with a taste exact, yet unconfin'd;
1   2   3 || 4   5

A knowledge both of books and human kind;
    1   2   3 || 4   5

Gen'rous converse; a soul exempt from pride;
    1   2 || 3   4   5

And love to praise, with reason on his side?
    1   2 || 3   4   5

Some of these lines have clearer cesuras than others, and some may be scanned with two or more cesuras, others with none. Cesuras, like promotions and demotions, are often dependent on the individual's ear. Some metrists, for example, may record no cesura at all in the eighth line.

Part of a poet's performance involves his ability to give variety to his cadences, phrases, and ideas by moving toward and away from strong cesuras, either illuminating the two-part construction of his lines or else fading it out entirely. Here is a demonstration of the use of the cesura:

Born but to die, and reas'ning but to err;
Alike in ignorance, his reason such,

Whether he thinks too little, or too much:
Chaos of Thought and Passion, all confus'd;
Still by himself abus'd, or disabus'd;
Created half to rise, and half to fall;
Great lord of all things, yet a prey to all;
Sole judge of Truth, in endless Error hurl'd:
The glory, jest, and riddle of the world!

The cesura helps to create an environment in which meters can perform. It is not strictly part of the meter itself: it provides not the organization of rhythms, but the boundaries of organization. Metrists often record the cesura only where it is clearly helpful to the scansion or necessary to an understanding of the meter being analyzed. Here, as with all the other metrical symbols and terms, usefulness is the criterion, to be determined by the analyst's needs at any given moment. In some poems the cesura always occurs at a fixed position in the line, thus providing a place where special metrical effects can be anticipated.

NORM LINE

We have seen that the meter of a certain poem is merely a generalization and simplification of the pattern into which the actual rhythms will *tend* to fall, so far as we can predict. It is possible, therefore, that the scansion of no single line in the poem will exactly match the *over-all* metrical design; each one may contain some kind of variation. A **norm line** is simply a scansion that represents the theoretically perfect line.

We discover the norm line by determining the metrical principle that appears to control the actual rhythms. We look for the norm that the rhythms seem to qualify for most economically and completely.

The norm line, then, is two things, and serves the critic in two ways: (1) it is a generalization of the rhythmical patterns, a representation of the meter; and (2) it is a model that the rhythms appear to be following. We work with it in two steps: first, we look at the rhythms of the poem and develop from them an idea of the norm. Then we fix the norm in our minds as a stable point of reference, and regard the variations in the actual rhythms as *departures from* the norm.

Determining the norm line is not often a laborious operation: we usually work mentally and quickly, instead of undertaking a series of penciled computations, corrections, and re-computations. What follows, therefore, is a greatly magnified, slow motion description of the *kinds* of decisions that may be involved, consciously, semi-consciously, or instinctively, in this process.

Let us imagine that we have given a passage of poetry the following *rhythmic* scansion:

```
1 — x x — x — x — x —
2 x — — x x — x — x —
3 x — x — — x x — x —
4 x — x — x — — x x —
5 x — x — — x x — x — x
6 x — — x x — x — x —
```

Developing a norm line out of this means finding a *pattern* of stresses and slacks that will be as clear, consistent, simple, and complete as possible. There are many ways of arriving at such a pattern. Sometimes it emerges clearly without effort, but at other times we need to analyze the data. Here is one possible way of making such an analysis:

(1) *Determine what all the lines have in common*, if anything. In this case, they all contain five stresses.

(2) *Determine what most of the lines have in common*, if anything. Inspection shows that, out of the 6 given lines:

    a) 5 begin with a slack
    b) 5 end with a stress
    c) 5 are made of ten syllables

d) 5 contain five slacks while an unusual line of eleven syllables contains six slacks. Therefore (since all contain five stresses), slacks and stresses are as evenly divided as is arithmetically possible.

We can now proceed on the hypothesis that the norm line for this poem will probably contain ten syllables, evenly dividing stresses and slacks, and will begin with a slack and end with a stress.

(3) *Determine what patterns seem to be repeated, or what the limitations of patterning are, or what features are particularly striking*, if any. Our discovery that the stresses and slacks are equally divided should make us consider a one-to-one ratio for them, a pairing-off. This should become an even stronger possibility when we realize that nowhere in the poem do we have more than two consecutive stresses or slacks; every stress adjoins a slack on at least one side, and every slack a stress. Furthermore, most of the stresses and slacks occur in regular alternation. So let us hypothesize a basic unit consisting of one stress and one slack. But in what order? The first two syllables of the passage indicate that the stress should come first: |− x|. When we try out this pattern in the entire line, however, it becomes complicated and unclear: the third syllable would have to be taken as an exception and omitted, while the final unit would be without a slack:

$$- x \mid x - x \mid - x \mid - x \mid -$$

Our alternative is: |x −|. This is, indeed, more reasonable, since, as we have already discovered, the norm line will probably begin with a slack and end with a stress. Momentarily ignoring the first two syllables of the poem as possible variants, then, we make our new unit divisions, or feet:

1 (− x)| x − | x − | x − | x −

2 x − | − x | x − | x − | x −

3 x − | x − | − x | x − | x −

4 x − | x − | x − | − x | x −

5 x − | x − | − x | x − | x − | x

(4) *Test the proposed pattern against the rhythmical scansion.* We find that the scansion serves well to explain the rhythmical organization of nearly the entire passage. Except for the extra eleventh syllable in the fifth line, the structure is consistent: each line consists of five units, each composed of one stress and one slack. Of the 30 feet in the poem, 24 (80 per cent) take the pattern |x −|. The remaining 6 all take the pattern |− x|. Thus, in the scansion we have chosen, each line has four regular feet and one **variation** foot or **substitution**.

(5) *Determine the nature and extent of predictable elements.* On the basis of the analyzed passage we conclude that, if the poet continues in the same kind of meter, it should fall into units of the |x −| pattern about 80 per cent of the time and into the |− x| pattern about 20 per cent of the time.

The *variation*, then, is not at all insignificant. It occurs so frequently that it seems to be part of the meter. In certain meters, certain variations come almost to belong to the norm, as an amendment becomes part of a law.

But what place in the line ought to contain the variant foot? In our sample, the *substitution* occurs in every place except the last, and in no particular order, at least not enough to contribute to the predictable pattern. So we may conclude that a substitution is likely to occur approximately once per line, but we cannot say *where* in the line it will fall except that it will probably not fall at the last foot.

So a statement about the meter of the poem would be something like this: the typical line consists of five feet, four of them having the |x −| pattern and one, which may occur in any position except the last, having the |— x| pattern. There is also some possibility of an extra slack at the end of the line. How are we to diagram this? If we render the norm line as

— x | x — | x — | x — | x —

we give the impression that the substitution always begins the line. The truth is that we cannot diagram the substitute foot as part of the norm line because it has no fixed place. The line that best summarizes the over-all metrical tendency of the passage *ignores* the variations and is rendered:

x — | x — | x — | x — | x —

This preserves, or even crystallizes, the major characteristics of the data: ten syllables composed of five stresses alternating with five slacks in a pattern predominantly |x —|. It so happens that this particular meter as used in English has traditionally allowed the substitution of the |— x| unit, which, since it is the reverse of the |x —| norm, is also called an **inversion** or **inverted foot**. As we come to recognize the traditional metrical forms we will also come to expect standard variations of this sort.

The foot-scansion given above under (3) recorded only five of the six lines. Have we developed, out of these five lines, a norm that will help us to predict the organization of the sixth line? The rhythmic scansion of that line was:

x — — x x — x — x —

Now, using our norm line as a guide, or mold, or *matrix*, we mark out the divisions to arrive at the metrical scansion:

x — | — x | x — | x — | x —

As the norm predicted, the sixth line contains ten syllables, slacks pairing off with stresses in a predominantly |x —| pattern. The only variant is an inversion in the second foot, which we have come to expect. The final test of a workable scansion, predictability, has been adequately successful. We have now developed a norm line that efficiently describes the general organization of the rhythms and that helps us in our scansion of further lines. It is important to remember, as this sample illustrates, that the metrical *norm* and the *scansion* are not necessarily identical.

COUNTERPOINT

The term **counterpoint**, for better or worse, has come into general use to describe the idea that the "rhythm" of a poem is actually an interplay between the prose rhythm and the meter. Counterpoint means, from the musical analogy, the presence of two or more melodies at the same time. We are not able to recite two rhythms at the same time, but we can convey some sense of their interplay by compromising between them. The compromise is recorded in our scansion.

Counterpoint, in other words, describes the poet's tendency to pull his rhythms away from a metrical pattern—within reasonable limits. He must not go so far that the reader forgets the meter lying behind the actual rhythms. The tension that has to be maintained continually between rhythm and meter can exist only if we remain aware of both conflicting elements, just as, in music, a "variation on a theme" requires the listener to remember the original melody while he hears the variations upon it. If the actual rhythms should deviate so much that we can no longer remember the meter as a point of reference, the tension ceases to exist. It is like the mainspring of a watch: the tension is maintained so long as one end of the mainspring is attached to a fixed point (the meter), and the other is attached to a movable part (the rhythm). If the movable part is made to go too far, the spring breaks loose and the entire tension is discharged. This results in **sprung rhythm**, a rhythm sprung out of tension with a controlling metrical norm. A poem of sprung rhythm, then, is one in which any "patterning" of stresses exists only in the immediate, actual rhythm, without reference to any restrictive, controlling meter.

A poem where the contrapuntal tension between rhythm and meter is maintained is said to be in **running rhythm**: the spring tension is maintained and the clock is running properly.

In any line, we may find either more or fewer clear prose stresses than the meter requires, meaning that we need to promote or demote some of them. A line that, in the prose pronunciation, contains more stresses than the meter requires is said to have a greater **density**, or to be more metrically dense, than a line with fewer stresses. One way of recording the degree of density is to divide the number of prose stresses in the line by the number of stresses demanded by the meter, to arrive at the *coefficient of density*. Let us assume that both lines below have been established as belonging to a metrical pattern that requires each line to have five stresses:

rhythmical
stresses   1   2   3   4   4
            Of Mans First Disobedience, and the Fruit $\frac{-}{-} = .8$
metrical   –   –   –   ⌢   –   5
stresses

                 1   2   3   4   5   6   6
            With head, hands, wings, or feet pursues his way $\frac{-}{-} = 1.2$
                 –   –   –   –   –   5

The coefficient of density in the first line is .8, in the second 1.2. It is a workable device only in running rhythm because only running rhythm consistently exploits this kind of tension.

RISING AND FALLING

The terms rising rhythm and falling rhythm are sometimes applied to metrical feet and sometimes to the rhythms of the words. In both cases, **rising** means moving from slack to stress, while **falling** means moving from stress to slack. The statement that a poem is written in rising rhythm normally means that the basic metrical foot is a rising one. The word-rhythm can either parallel or contrast with it. In the line

    Away! Away! Away!
    x − |x − |x −

the metrical foot and the word "away" are both in rising rhythm. The situation is different in

metrical rhythm   x −| x −| x −|x −| x −
                     As after sunset fadeth in the west
word-rhythm |− x|− x| − x |

where the meter has a perfect rising rhythm, while three key words (comprising 60 per cent of the line) are in falling rhythm.

DIFFERENTIAL

The difference in *degree* of emphasis between slack and stressed syllables in a line is sometimes worth noting, and for it we can use the term **differential**. There is a relatively small differential in the line

    To love that well which thou must leave ere long
    x − | x   −| x   −| x − |x −

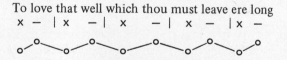

We find more prominent stress differences, though still a fairly small total differential, in

    Unréspited, unpitied, unrepreevd
    x −| x − | x −|x   − |x   −

But the differential is large and clear in

And swims or sinks, or wades, or creeps, or flyes
x   — | x — | x   — | x   — | x —

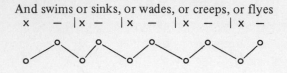

MODALITY

In the type of English meter that uses feet, the basic unit (foot) is composed of one stress accompanied either by one or by two slacks. We can call these the two main rhythmic **modes** or **modalities**, consisting of the **duple rhythms** of two-syllable units (x — and — x) and the **triple rhythms** of three-syllable units (xx — and — xx). Sometimes a poem in one modality will admit a segment in the other modality freely, sometimes only as an exception, and sometimes not at all.

It is possible to create the appearance of changing modalities when in fact preserving the original one. We start with a meter in perfect duple rhythm:

x — | x — | x — | x — | x —
1 2 3 4 5 6 7 8 9 10

Now let us substitute two inverted feet, say the first and third of the line. Since we merely transpose the feet we preserve the metrical one-to-one ratio between stresses and slacks,

inversion   *inversion*
       | |
— x | x — | — x | x — | x —
1 2   3 4   5 6   7 8   9 10   (5 stresses, 5 slacks)

yet we have achieved the *rhythmical* illusion of a *triple* mode
in two places:

rhythmically triple mode
(ratio: 2 slacks to 1 stress)

— x x — — x x — x —   *metrically duple mode*
  2 3 4   6 7 8   *(ratio: 1 stress to 1 slack)*

This is another dimension for the poet to move in. It is
another way that he enjoys *rhythmical* freedom while strictly
obeying *metrical* law.

When a rhythm shifts at random from one mode to another,
it is a **duple-triple rhythm**:

Fear no more the frown o' the great;
—   x   —   x   —   x   x   —

duple   duple   triple

Thou art past the tyrant's stroke.
x   x   —   x   —   x   —

triple   duple   duple

Duple-triple refers only to the rhythm, not to the meter.
When, metrically, there is a significant shift from duple to
triple *feet*, or from triple to duple, we can refer to it as **modal
shift**. Modal shift is therefore cited in cases of a noticeable
disruption of an established ratio between stresses and slacks.
Duple-triple rhythm describes a continual, arbitrary shifting
of such ratios. Duple-triple is a type of rhythm; modal shift
is a sudden change in the metrical design.

TYPES OF METER

The business of scansion would be very much simplified if
all English poems followed the same kind of metrical system.

But they do not, and some of them resist being scanned under any sort of metrical regularity whatever (see Chapter VI). When confronted with a poem, we need to decide which system of scansion will be most useful for our purposes. Some of the terms and symbols presented in this chapter will prove to be more directly pertinent to one type of meter than to another.

There are three main families or types of meter in English, with various subtypes:

(1) *Syllabic Verse*. The significant element is simply the total number of syllables in the line of poetry, regardless of which are stressed and which are slack. The syllable-count per line is relatively predictable. (This type is the subject of Chapter V.)

(2) *Stress-Verse*. The significant element is the number of *stresses* in the line. Thus a distinction is made between some syllables and others, and the focus is put on the stresses, which are accordingly the "markers" for the metrical demands of the line. There are two major subtypes of stress-verse:

> a) *simple stress-verse* merely counts the total number of stresses in the line. The stress-count is relatively predictable. (Chapter III)

> b) *the native meters* include one very large branch of metrical organization, *folk meter*. Folk meter takes into account not only the number of stresses per line, but also their position regarding a fixed cesura, the relationship between secondary and primary stresses, and another very special feature: a *pause* that can substitute for a stress. These folk meters, in their various guises, are important, complex, and prevalent enough to deserve a chapter to themselves. (Chapter IV)

(3) *Foot-Verse*. The significant elements are the number of stresses per line, the number of slacks (and hence the total number of syllables), the ratio of slacks to stresses, and the

forms into which the slacks and stresses tend to cluster. Because the concern is for all syllables within the line as well as for the stress "markers," this type of meter is also called *syllable-stress verse*. It is the most detailed, as well as the most traditional, form of metrical scansion, the "school-room" method. Some of the technical features that were discussed in this chapter pertain only to foot-verse. (Chapter II)

It is important to remember that these three main families of meter overlap a great deal. Meter, after all, is a way of describing the rhythmical organization of poetry, and most poems can be described in more than one way. A poem in foot-verse, containing five feet per line, is also describable as stress-verse because each line will contain five stresses. The overlapping relationship between the three forms may be diagrammed as follows:

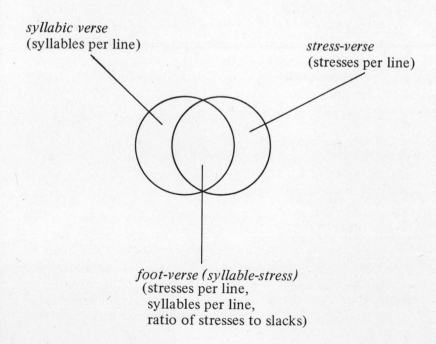

syllabic verse
(syllables per line)

stress-verse
(stresses per line)

foot-verse (syllable-stress)
(stresses per line,
syllables per line,
ratio of stresses to slacks)

Sometimes, then, we will need to decide which type of meter to use in scanning a poem, and our choice will depend on the sort of information we want to get. For example, the lines

The curfew tolls the knell of parting day,

The lowing herd wind slowly o'er the lea

are completely regular as to their number of syllables, the number of stresses and slacks per line, and the number and type of metrical feet. They could be used as examples of all three main types of meter. If we were to scan them as syllabic verse, pointing out that each line contains ten syllables, we would be saying nothing about the stresses. If we described them as simple stress-verse, we would be ignoring the regularity of the syllable-counts and the steady rhythmic alternation of stresses and slacks. We can convey most information about these lines by using the terminology of foot-verse; this would produce the most "elegant" description, providing we did not wish purposely to limit the focus to the stress-count or syllable-count.

There is no point in trying to make the main types of meter mutually exclusive. To insist, for example, that a poem cannot be syllabic verse *because* it is stress-verse is misleading. We classify types of meter because we want to illuminate important differences between poems, but we should not therefore refuse to see their equally important similarities, or fail to appreciate the poem that can qualify under different metrical systems with equal ease.

The overlapping of metrical types is particularly important in the classification of folk meters, which we regard as stress-verse even though some of the labels used for them (*e.g.*, "Common Meter," "Poulter's Measure") originally applied to syllabic forms. These forms happen to contain distinctive and dependable stress-patterns that are fundamentally similar to other clear stress-verse forms. Their syllabic regularity proves to be less significant than their stress-patterns, and this makes it useful to regard them as stress-verse despite their historical origins. Scansion, again, is a critic's tool, for which the test must be convenience and clarity.

CHAPTER II
FOOT-VERSE (SYLLABLE-STRESS VERSE)

Foot-verse is the most detailed meter in English and has produced the largest system of technical terms and labels. These enable us to summarize economically what we find to be the rhythmic nature of the norm line, its modality, the number of its stresses and slacks and their relative position, the variations common to it, some of its potentials for other variations and special effects, and the general poetic tradition to which it belongs.

The province of foot-verse can be illustrated by comparing it with the other two types described at the end of the previous chapter, syllabic verse and stress-verse:

(1) When we scan a poem as *syllabic verse*, we are concerned only with the total number of syllables in the line:

	syllables
No motion has she now, no force;	
1 2 3 4 5 6 7 8	8
She neither hears nor sees;	
1 2 3 4 5 6	6
Rolled round in earth's diurnal course,	
1 2 3 4 5 6 7 8	8
With rocks, and stones, and trees.	
1 2 3 4 5 6	6

(2) We may scan the same poem as *stress-verse* and be concerned only with the total number of stresses in the line:

	stresses
No mótion hás she nów, no fórce;	4
She néither héars nor sées,	3
Rolled róund in eárth's diúrnal cóurse,	4
With rócks, and stónes, and trées.	3

(3) But the most fruitful approach would be to scan this poem as *foot-verse*. We see that in this case, at least, something consistent can be said of the number, placement, and relationship of both stresses and slacks:

	type and number of units or "feet"
No motion has she now, no force; x — |x — |x — | x —	4 (x —)
She neither hears nor sees; x — | x — | x —	3 (x —)
Rolled round in earth's diurnal course, x̂ — |x — | x–|x —	4 (x —)
With rocks, and stones, and trees. x — |x — | x —	3 (x —)

Notice that the number of feet in each line is the same as the number of stresses in the stress-verse scansion, and that each foot has only one stress. This is a main principle, and without it foot-scansion would be far less useful. Let us restate it as one of the basic assumptions of metrical theory:

> In foot-verse scansion, the foot normally contains exactly one stress, neither more nor less. It may contain one, two, or sometimes three slacks, and sometimes no slacks at all, in which case it is a deficient foot.

(The only practical exception to this rule is the ionic double-foot, discussed later.)

Other definitions of the foot have been tried but have not proved as useful as this one. It is good to be reminded here that a useful system of scansion must be a compromise, indicating both actual rhythms and abstract principles of organization. We could construct a very simple system containing only two feet, one consisting of one stress and the other of one slack. With this system we could "scan" every poem in our language, but it would not be very useful or interesting because it would not sufficiently generalize about the rhythms or give a sense of pattern or of tension. On the other hand, we could construct a system using many long and complicated foot patterns, but here again we would not benefit by them because they would not reduce the rhythms to workably simple terms. The most useful kind of scansion follows the principle of *applying the simplest pattern that will do the required job.*

Our scansion of poetry uses a large number of the concepts and terms used in the scansion of Greek and Latin poetry. Some persons object that these classical terms are not literally applicable to English. We should keep in mind, however, that (1) we need to borrow only those concepts that are useful to our own purposes, using them as analogies if not literally, and that (2) this borrowed system has proved itself more useful than any other in describing certain kinds of rhythmic organization.

The system of foot-verse scansion set forth here gives the basic patterns, and upon them builds a superstructure of variations, exceptions, special instances. We are interested in the metrical departures a poet makes from the norm, so we want to be able to codify these departures as much as we profitably can.

The criteria for establishing the meter of foot-verse are:

(1) The basic *foot* in the line, seen as the most efficient grouping of stresses and slacks into clusters. The foot is a unit of rhythmic features, not of meaning, and does not depend on word or phrase boundaries.

(2) The number of feet in the basic line, the norm line. The principle here is to determine the one kind of foot that will best qualify as the norm, and to take other kinds of feet as exceptions to it.

(3) Sometimes, the pattern made by a group of lines. It may be continuous, one line following another for an indefinite period, or it may be divided by rhyme, rhythm, or other device into line-batches of two, three, and so on, up to the larger units such as odes, sonnets, and special stanzas.

THE NORMS OF FOOT-VERSE

Feet

Tradition and convenience have established four basic feet in English:

	duple rhythm ↓	*triple rhythm* ↓
rising rhythm ⟶	iambic (x −)	anapestic (xx −)
falling rhythm ⟶	trochaic (− x)	dactylic (− xx)

The Iamb, or Iambic Foot

This consists of a relatively lesser-stressed syllable followed by a relatively greater-stressed one, or a syllable that counts metrically as slack followed by one that counts metrically as stress. For simplicity we may say that an iamb consists of one slack followed by one stress, symbolized | x − | :

I met a pig
x − |x −   2 (x −)

Without a wig
x − |x −   2 (x −)

In all four feet here the foot boundaries come at word boundaries. But this is coincidence or artistry. One of the uses of scansion, indeed, is to dramatize how foot and word boundaries can proceed independently, yet manage to con- clude together at the end of the line. When a word and a foot end at the same syllable it is **dieresis;** when a word runs over the metrical boundary from one foot into another it is **linkage,** the **linking** of feet by words. The scansion of dieresis or linkage depends entirely on what we choose to establish as the **staple,** the basic meter of that particular poem or line. In the following iambic line, the second and third feet are linked while the first, third, fourth, and fifth feet exemplify dieresis:

> When I consider how my light is spent
> x −| x −|x − | x − |x −.   5 (x −)
>   ‿
> |
>   linking

The Trochee, or Trochaic Foot

The **trochaic foot** has one stress followed by one slack, symbolized | − x | :

> Werther had a love for Charlotte, such as words could never utter;
> − x | − x|− x | − x |− x | −   x | −x |− x
>   8 (− x)

> Would you know how first he met her? she was cutting bread
> −   x | − x | − x| − x | − x | − x | −

> and butter.
> x | − x   8 (− x)

Trochaic meters generally have less linkage than iambic ones. The passage above contains dieresis throughout. Note that in both lines the cesura falls after the fourth foot, dividing the line exactly in half.

There are only two linkages in this passage:

> What, there's nothing in the moon noteworthy?
> −   x   − x ⁀ x — x̂ | − x

> Nay: for if that moon could love a mortal,
> −   x − x — x − x − x

> Use, to charm him (so to fit a fancy),

All her magic ('tis the old sweet mythos),

She would turn a new side to her mortal,

Side unseen of herdsman, huntsman, steersman.
— x | —

The desire to give strong endings to lines, by rhyme or in some other way, frequently leads in staple trochaic meter to omission of the last slack in the line, in order to conclude on a stress. In such cases the last foot is said to be **deficient** or, more technically, **catalectic:**

1 Tell me not, in mournful numbers,
     —   x| — x | —   x | —   x   4 (— x)

2 Life is but an empty dream! —
     — x| — x |— x | ——   4 (— x)   *catalectic*

3 For the soul is dead that slumbers,
     — x| — x| —   x | — x   4 (— x)

4 And things are not what they seem.
     —̱ x̂ | — x | — x | ——   4 (— x)   *catalectic*
     x   — |

You may choose, in line 4 here, to substitute an iamb for the first trochee, but that would mean destroying the established heavy regularity of evenly alternating stresses and slacks in perfect duple rhythm. It would bring two slacks together (the last syllable of line 3 and the first of line 4), thus swinging into a triple rhythm that might seem incongruous in a context of such heavy duples. The metrical **context,** or larger rhythmic and metrical environment, is important again in our *determination* of the two catalectic lines. Instead of trochaics with the last slack missing, they could easily be scanned as iambics with the first slack missing: |() —|x —|x —|x —|. Sometimes the choice is quite arbitrary. In this case, however, the context of the first and third lines should lead us to decide on a trochaic norm.

The Anapest, or Anapestic Foot

The **anapest** is the triple-rhythm counterpart of the iamb; it consists of *two* slacks followed by one stress, symbolized | xx — |:

> The Assyrian came down like the wolf on the fold,
> x x —|x x   — |x   x   — |x x —   4 (xx —)
>
> And his cohorts were gleaming in purple and gold;
> x   x —|x   x   — | x x — |x   x   —   4 (xx —)
>
> And the sheen of their spears was like stars on the sea,
>
> When the blue wave rolls nightly on deep Galilee.

One or even both of the slacks at the beginning of the anapestic line are sometimes omitted, creating a **headless** or **acephalous** line. This process is called **truncation.** The second line of the following stanza of anapestics is halfway truncated:

> I am monarch of all I survey;
> x x   —
>
> My right there is none to dispute;
> x —
>
> From the centre all round to the sea
> x   x   —
>
> I am lord of the fowl and the brute.
> x x   —

Another variation frequently found in anapestics is the substitution of an iamb for an anapest, creating a momentary slowing of the pace from triple to duple rhythm and providing strong counterpoint to the anapestic staple. Notice the iambic substitutions in this anapestic passage:

iambic substitutions

	No.	Place

Let it flame or fade, and the war roll down like a
x x − |x − | x   x   −| x̂ − |x x

wind,   2   2,4
−

We have proved we have hearts in a cause, we are
x x   − | x x   − |x x − | x x

noble still,
− |x −   1   5

And myself have awaked, as it seems, to the better
x   x − | x   x − |x x − | x x −|x

mind;
−   1   5

It is better to fight for the good than to rail at
x x −| x x − | x   x   — | x   x −| x

the ill;
x −   0   −

I have felt with my native land, I am one with
x x   − | x   x −|x − |x x − | x

my kind,
x −   1   3

I embrace the purpose of God, and the doom
x x   − | x −|x   x − | x x   — |

assign'd.
x −   2   2,5

The passage contains 30 feet, of which 23 are anapests, which means that the anapest norm is maintained about 77 per cent of the time. This is particularly interesting here, because not a single line begins with an iambic substitution. It is almost as though the poet wanted us to be sure to start out on the proper foot. Yet only the fourth line is entirely "normal."

The Dactyl, or Dactylic Foot

This is the triple-rhythm counterpart of the trochee; it consists of one stress followed by two slacks, symbolized |− xx|:

After the pangs of a desperate lover
− x x |−   x x| − x x | − x   4 (− xx) *catalectic*

When day and night I have sighed all in vain;
−   x̂   x |−   x x |−   x x |−   4 (− xx) *double catalectic*

Ah, what a pleasure it is to discover
−   x x| − x x|− x x | − x   4 (− xx) *catalectic*

In her eyes pity, who causes my pain!
− x x̂ |−x   x | − x   x| −   4 (− xx) *double catalectic*

Dactylic meter is the rarest of the four staples and almost never appears without some substitutions or catalexes. Poems that could be scanned with a dactylic base often have so many exceptions and variations that it is more economical to regard them as stress-verse. Even the above example, a relatively "pure" dactylic, is deficient in the final foot of every line, or 25 per cent of the time (4 deficient feet out of 16). Because the stresses, in this triple rhythm, are separated by two slacks, they are more prominent than they would be in duple rhythms: triple rhythms usually have a greater *differential.*

The concepts of linkage and dieresis may be of value in discussing some passages of dactylics or anapestics, but their effect is not usually as striking as in the tighter contexts of iambic or trochaic feet. Triple meters tend to draw our attention away from foot boundaries and towards the heavy recurring stresses. That is, slack syllables are less noticeable in triple rhythms than in duples, so that we are less conscious of foot divisions.

Feet Used in Variation Only

Metrists from time to time have allowed special "feet" into their systems of scansion. We must do so with a good deal of caution. There is a danger in allowing exceptions more often than necessary. Overly free substitution of nonstaple feet weakens the organizing principle, and leaves us no way of determining how closely the poet follows a certain pattern.
Let us take a line that scans:

x – x – – x x – x –

This could be seen as two iambs, plus one dactyl, plus one trochee, plus a final trochee catalectic:

x – | x – | – x x | – x | – ( )

Or it could be taken as two iambs, plus a third iamb minus its slack, plus an anapest, plus an iamb:

x – | x – | ( ) – | x x – | x –

Here we have created a new kind of exceptional foot: a deficient iamb within the line, not merely at the beginning of it. We could easily create other feet consisting of more than one stress or of no stresses, or of stresses surrounded by slacks, or the other way around, producing such scansions as:

x – x | – – | x x | – x –

or

x | – x – | – x x | – x –

and so forth. But by now the point of scanning the line seems to have been lost. What are we trying to achieve? If the purpose of scansion is to indicate at least to some degree the (1) norm behind the rhythm and (2) the deviation from the norm, these samples are of little help because they do not indicate a norm. The most useful approach is through the principle of *using the standard wherever possible*, making the pattern as simple and consistent as the rhythm will allow and adhering to our basic definition of a foot as containing exactly one stress:

$$x - | x - | - x | x - | x -$$

This describes the rhythm as being organized into a line that tends toward five iambs but has one trochee substituted for an iamb.

What are the advantages of such a restrictive scansion? We preserve our definition of the foot. We indicate some contrapuntal techniques: the line rhythmically has two stresses coming together at one place and two slacks in another, creating a sense of triple rhythm while the scansion shows that metrically there has been no break in modality. We indicate that the poet produces a sense of freedom in rhythmic movement while yet adhering strictly to the metrical law (here) of exactly one slack to be assigned to every stress: the entire line contains exactly five stresses and five slacks. Also, we minimize the terminology, dealing with only the staple foot and one standard variation rather than, as in some of the alternate scansions, with four different complex feet. If this line were to occur, as it frequently does, in the context of the five-foot iambic line, our restrictive scansion would preserve the five-foot norm. All this should indicate the need for caution in deciding to bring special variant feet into the scansion of foot-verse.

The Ionic (Rising, Ascending, Lesser Ionic) Foot. Of all the special feet, only the ionic is practical. Although it does in a sense violate the rule that the foot may have only one stress, it compensates by representing two feet: it is a *double foot* composed of *two* slacks followed by *two* stresses, symbolized | x x − − |:

In confus'd march forlorn, th' adventrous Bands

x   x   —   — | x — | x   — | x   —
     1,   2   3   4   5   *feet*

or

And sat as Princes, whom the supreme King

x   — | x — | x   — | x x   —   —
     1   2   3   4,   5   *feet*

We will return to the ionic in our discussion of substitutions.

Other Variant Feet (*"Cadences"*). The other feet used as special variations are perhaps unnecessary, and scansions that include them usually obscure rather than illuminate a pattern, often to such a degree that the scansion gives us little more than a simplified transcription of the rhythm. These "feet" are sometimes resorted to by metrists who are mainly concerned with rendering the *prose rhythm* of the poem.

pyrrhic:	Two slacks: | x x |
spondee:	Two stresses: | — — |
amphibrach:	| x — x |
amphimacer:	| — x — |
bacchic:	| x — — |
antibacchic:	| — — x |
tribrach:	| x x x |
molossus:	| — — — |
first paeon:	| — x x x |
second paeon:	| x — x x |
third paeon:	| x x — x |
fourth paeon:	| x x x — |
di-iamb:	| x — x — |

di-trochee: | — x — x |
choriamb: | — x x — |
antispast: | x — — x |
di-spondee: | — — — — |

Two of the most frequent rhythmical cadences in foot-verse are |—xx—| and |xx——|, the choriamb and the ascending ionic. In our scansion we will want to break up the choriamb into the standard trochee plus iamb, thereby communicating the sense that the first is a substitution, a simple *inversion*, of the second. But we will not break up the ionic because that would render a pyrrhic plus spondee, neither of which is a true foot. At times pyrrhics and spondees may seem the easiest way to scan a passage. But their use hinders us from discovering the true strictness of the meter and also obscures an important point: within these feet, one of the syllables will almost always be at least slightly stronger than the other $(x\acute{-})$, $(\acute{-}x)$, $(-\hat{x})$, or $(\hat{x}-)$. So when we render pyrrhics and spondees as iambs or trochees (with appropriate promotions or demotions) we get a sharper sense of the subtle shadings in the differential. Moreover, pyrrhics and spondees very often occur together in English poetry, creating the |xx——| pattern already accounted for by the ionic foot.

Lines

So far we have been concerned only with the types of metrical *feet* used in foot-verse scansion. Now, to arrive at the *meter* of a foot-verse poem, we must determine how *many* feet of which type are normally contained in the poetic line.

If the line has 1 foot it is **monometer**
            2 ”   **dimeter**
            3 ”   **trimeter**
            4 ”   **tetrameter**
            5 ”   **pentameter**
            6 ”   **hexameter**
            7 ”   **heptameter**
            8 ”   **octameter**

Thus, if we are faced with:

x — | x x — | x x —

x x — | x — | x x —

we would be fairly safe in identifying the meter as *anapestic trimeter*, although two of the six feet are iambic variations. The main types of foot-verse meters used in English will be used as illustrations throughout the rest of this chapter.

EXCEPTIONS TO THE REGULARITY OF FOOT-VERSE

One of the reasons for determining the meter of a poem is to become aware of the rhythmical variations upon it. Through the poetic cadences we get an idea of a general form, and we then look for the attempts to break away from it: we want to see what will happen to the meter under various conditions. Many of the variations in foot-verse have become standard, established through usage as legitimate amendments to the general metrical rules. We can now examine the main forms of these variations. Since iambic pentameter is the strictest line in foot-verse, we will use it as our example wherever possible.

In the Length of the Line

The length of the line can be changed in a number of ways without affecting the internal metrical structure. The most common way has been the addition or subtraction of syllables at the beginning or end of the line. This applies to slack syllables only, since any change in the number of stresses would mean, according to our definition of the foot, a change in the basic meter.

At the End of the Line

Catalexis. Catalexis is the omission of the last slack syllable in the line. Since rising meters normally end with a stress, catalexis is properly applicable only to the trochaic and dactylic meters.

Dactylic dimeter: 2(−xx)

> Cannon to right of them,
> − x x| − x x
>
> Cannon to left of them,
> − x x| − x x
>
> Cannon in front of them
> − x x | − x x
>
> Volley'd and thunder'd.
> − x x | − x   *catalectic*

(In dactylic meters, one or both of the final slacks in the line may be omitted.)

The catalectic line can also be used either consecutively or or in alternation with complete, or **acatalectic**, lines:

Trochaic trimeter: 3(−x)

> Taffy was a Welshman,
> − x | − x | − x
>
> Taffy was a thief;
> − x | − x | −   *catalectic*
>
> Taffy came to my house
> − x | − x | − x
>
> And stole a piece of beef.
> x | − x | − x | −   *catalectic*

(The final line might be considered iambic, but the first three lines have established a strong trochaic staple. "And" is an "anacrusis.")

Trochaic tetrameter catalectic: 4(−x)

> On a day−alack the day!−
> − x | − x | − x | −
>
> Love, whose month is ever May,
> − x | − x | − x | −

Spied a blossom passing fair
$-$ x| $-$ x | $-$ x | $-$

Playing in the wanton air.
$-$ x | $-$ x | $-$ x | $-$

Hypercatalexis. Hypercatalexis is the *addition* of a slack syllable at the end of the line, and we may expect to find it mostly in the rising meters. Hypercatalexes are sometimes more simply referred to as **feminine endings**, feminine in versification meaning "ending with a slack syllable." A line containing hypercatalexis may also be said to have **redundance** or to be **extrametrical** or **hypermetrical**, since the additional syllable does not belong to the regular syllabic count of the line.

Iambic tetrameter: 4(x$-$)

No more with overflowing light
x $-$ | x $-$|x $-$|x $-$

Shall fill the eyes that now are faded,
x $-$| x $-$ | x $-$ | x $-$|x   *hypercatalectic*

Nor shall another's fringe with night
                                        x $-$

Their woman-hidden world as they did.
                          x $-$ | x   *hypercatalectic*

Anapestic dimeter hypercatalectic

   or

Anapestic dimeter with feminine ending:

He is gone on the mountain,
x x $-$ | x   x $-$ | x

He is lost to the forest,
  x   x $-$ | x x $-$| x

Like a summer-dried fountain,

When our need was the sorest.

Iambic pentameter:

For solitude somtimes is best societie,

x —|x — |x   — |x   — |x — |x   *feminine ending*

And short retirement urges sweet returne.

(Note that "societie" and "retirement" are each to be pronounced with three syllables.)

Iambic pentameter:

'Tis heavy with him. And am I then revenged
x   — | x x   — | x   — |x — |x —

To take him in the purging of his soul,
x   — | x ⌢ | x   —| x   ⌢ | x   —

When he is fit and seasoned, for his passage?
x   —|x — | x — |x   ⌢ | x — |x   *feminine ending*

(Notice the anapestic substitution in the first line.)
  We sometimes find *two* hypermetricals at the end of a line.
In such cases we might be tempted to promote the final slack,
if possible, to give an additional stress to the line; it will
depend on the strength of the norm to keep our scansion
down to the permitted number of syllables. Here is an
example of a pulling-away from the norm:

Iambic pentameter hypercatalectic:

1 Whatever ails me, now a-late especially,
   x —|x — | x   — |x —|x —|x x   *double fem. end.*

2 I can as well be hanged as refrain seeing her;
   x — | x —| x   — | x x —   —|x   x   *double fem. end.*

3 Some twenty times a day, nay, not so little,
x   − | x − | x − | x̂   − | x − | x   *fem. end.*

4 Do I force errands, frame ways and excuses
x x −   − | x   − | −   x | x − | x   *fem. end.*

(Notice the ionic substitutions in lines 2 and 4, and the trochaic substitution in line 4. If you prefer to read "(es)pecially" and "seeing her" as having only two syllables each, you will be able to scan more standard feminine endings throughout.)

At the Beginning of the Line

Anacrusis.   **Anacrusis** is the addition of a hypermetrical slack at the beginning of the line. It is found in all the staple meters except the anapestic, where it would theoretically cause an awkward three slacks at the beginning of the line. It has often been likened to the "upbeat" in musical rhythm, especially in falling meters, where the counting of the meter officially begins at the first stress. Some metrists use the term to refer to any slack beginning a line, so that any normal iambic or anapestic line would contain anacrusis. It is more useful, however, to reserve the term for cases where a slack is *added* to the norm.

Iambic trimeter hypercatalectic (feminine ending):

The mountain sheep are sweeter,
x   − | x   − | x   − | x

But the valley sheep are fatter.
anacrusis   x | x − | x   − | x − | x

(This could also be described as trochaic trimeter with anacrusis in the first line and double anacrusis in the second line.)

Iambic pentameter:

Thou call'dst me up at midnight to fetch dew
x   − | x − | x   − | x   x −   −

From the still-vexed Bermoothes, there she's hid.
x   x   —   — | x   — | x   — | x   —

The mariners all under hatches stowed,
x   — |x ⌢ |— x |x   — | x   —

Who, with a charm joined to their suffered labor,
—   x |x   — | —   x |x   — | x   — |x   *fem. end.*

I have left asleep. And for the rest o' the fleet
anacrusis   x | x   — |x   — | —   x | x   — |x   x   —

(The second line here begins with two slacks but is not an anacrusis because these slacks go to make up a complete ionic foot. The last line may be considered as having two anapests, both of which can be eliminated if "o' the" is pronounced as one syllable, and "I have" is pronounced as "I've.")

The anacrusis in this case amounts to an anapestic substitution. But the stricter iambic pentameters do not allow any trisyllabic substitutions, and in such cases it is better to refer to anacrusis alone.

Truncation. Truncation is the omission of a slack at the beginning of the line. It therefore occurs only in rising meters. (The term catalexis is sometimes also used here as well as at the end of the line.)

Anapestic tetrameter alternating with anapestic trimeter:

Believe me, if all those endearing young charms,
truncated   x   — | x x   — | x   x   — |x   x   —

Which I gaze on so fondly to-day,
x   x   — | x   x   — |x   x   —

Were to change by to-morrow, and fleet in my arms,
x   x   — | x x   — |x   x   — |x   x —

Like fairy-gifts fading away.
truncated   x   — |x   x   — |x   x —

Iambic pentameter:

Twelve year since, Miranda, twelve year since
truncated   − | x̂ − | x − | x   − | x̂ −

In the Types of Ending

The ends of foot-verse lines, and even the ends of major sections of lines, have often been particularly sensitive rhythmically, and usually are allowed special license for metrical variation.

A line concluding on a slack syllable is said to have a **feminine ending**. A line concluding on a stress, as in any regular iambic pentameter, is said to have a **masculine ending**. There are two kinds of masculine ending. If the final syllable is a primary or secondary stress, as it usually is in rising meters, it is a **strong ending**. If it is a tertiary stress that needs to be promoted to ictus for the sake of the meter, it is called a **weak ending** or **light ending**:

Iambic pentameter:

O sleep, thou ape of death, lie dull upon her,
       x − | x   *feminine ending*

And be her sense but as a monument,
      x − | x −̂   *light ending*

Thus in a chapel lying! Come off, come off.
       | x −

As slippery as the Gordian knot was hard!

'Tis mine, and this will witness outwardly,
     x − | x   −̂   *light ending*

As strongly as the conscience does within.

In iambic pentameter especially, the line-end and the cesura have many similar characteristics. The presence of the cesura depends on our sense of a break, or a logical pause, in the *meaning* of the words. This can make the very existence of the cesura a matter of opinion. A similar sense of logical division operates at the end of the line. When we feel that the last syllable brings a phrase to a definite sort of break or logical pause, we say that the line is **end-stopped** or **estopped**. When, however, the meaning of the words seems to run on into the next line without a noticeable break, thus uniting the two lines, it is said to be a **run-on line** by virtue of the activity called **enjambment**.

Iambic pentameter:

If I have too austerely punished you,	*estopped*
Your compensation makes amends. For I	*run-on*
Have given you here a third of mine own life,	*estopped*
Or that for which I live, who once again	*run-on*
I tender to thy hand. All thy vexations	*run-on*
Were but my trials of thy love, and thou	*run-on*
Hast strangely stood the test. Here, afore Heaven,	*estopped*
I ratify this my rich gift. O Ferdinand,	*estopped*
Do not smile at me that I boast her off,	*estopped*
For thou shalt find she will outstrip all praise.	*estopped*

When a passage of iambic pentameter avoids enjambment and renders every line more or less a logical unit in itself, thus shaping the content into clusters of five stresses and about ten syllables, it creates a form that is said to consist of **single-molded lines**.

The difference between enjambed and estopped lines is particularly important where the iambic pentameter is rhymed in pairs of lines, or couplets. When the second line of the couplet is enjambed, we have an **open couplet**; when it is estopped, we have a **closed couplet**:

Iambic pentameter couplets:

The rebels, as you heard, being driven hence,	*a* ⎤
Despairing e'er to expiate their offence	*a* ⎦ *open*

By a too late submission, fled to sea   *b* ⎤
In such poor barks as they could get, where they   *b* ⎦ *open*
Roamed up and down, which way the winds did please, *c* ⎤
Without a chart or compass: the rough seas   *c* ⎦ *open*
Enraged with such a load of wickedness,   *d* ⎤
Grew big with billows, great was their distress;   *d* ⎦*closed*
Yet was their courage greater; desperate men   *e* ⎤
Grow valianter with suffering: in their ken   *e* ⎦ *open*
Was a small island, thitherward they steer   *f* ⎤
Their weather-beaten barks, each plies his gear;   *f* ⎦*closed*
Some row, some pump, some trim the ragged sails,   *g* ⎤
All were employed and industry prevails.   *g* ⎦*closed*

In the Types of Division: The Cesura

Strictly speaking, the cesura is not part of the meter. But by creating line divisions, or **sections**, it provides a place where certain metrical effects can be achieved, much as at the line-ends, and some poets take as many metrical liberties at the cesura as are traditionally allowed at the end. In the case of a line with several cesuras, we can expect to find one stronger than the others, and it is at this place that the special metrical effects will ordinarily be found.

The stricter kind of cesura tends to come near the middle of the ten syllables of the iambic pentameter, thus breaking the line into approximately equal sections. If it comes after the fourth, fifth, or sixth syllable in the iambic pentameter it is a **medial cesura**. If it comes earlier or later it is a **variant cesura**. After a slack syllable it is a **feminine cesura**; after a stress, a **masculine cesura**.

Iambic pentameter: *after*
                                        type of   *syll.*
                                        cesura   *no.*

Ethereal Trumpet from on high gan blow:
            x ‖   *medial feminine*   5
At which command the Powers Militant,
            — ‖   *medial masculine*   4

	type of cesura	after syll. no.

That stood for Heav'n, in mighty Quadrate joyn'd

      – ‖   *medial masculine*   4

Of Union irresistible, mov'd on

      ‿̄ ‖   *variant masculine*   8

In silence thir bright Legions, to the sound

           x ‖   *variant feminine*   7

Of instrumental Harmonie that breath'd

      ‿̄ ‖   *variant masculine*   8

Heroic Ardor to advent'rous deeds

     x ‖   *medial feminine*   5

Under thir God-like Leaders, in the Cause.

        x ‖   *variant feminine*   7

In the iambic meters, the feminine cesura can be sub-classified into two types. Its normal occurrence, after a slack and before the next stress, would be in the middle of the iamb, dividing its two syllables. When the cesura cuts in this way through a foot of the metrical pattern, it is a **lyric cesura**.

Lyric cesura:

Trumpet from on high
  | x ‖ – |·

Legions, to the
  | x ‖ – |

Ardor to advent'rous
  | x ‖ – |

Leaders, in the
  |x ‖ – |

The other kind of feminine cesura appears when the poet adds a slack at the end of the first section of the line, creating a feminine ending hypermetrically, just as he might at the end of the full-line.   This addition, which results in an eleven-syllable line, creates an **epic cesura**.

When the iambic pentameter has a masculine cesura, the slack that ought to begin the second section of the line may be missing.   This is called a **truncated cesura**, leaving a nine-syllable line.

Iambic pentameter:

It shall be in eternal restless change

Self-fed, and self-consum'd, ‖ if this fail,

x̂   — | x   — | x   — | — | x   —   *truncated cesura*

The pillar'd firmament is rott'nness,

And earths base built on stubble. ‖ But com let's on.

x   — | x̂   — | x — | (x)   x   — | x   —   *epic cesura*

Against th' opposing will and arm of Heav'n

May never this just sword be lifted up,

But for that damn'd magician, ‖ let him be girt

x — | x   — | x —| (x)   — x | x —   *epic cesura*

With all the greisly legions that troop

Several interpretations of the metrical variations that occur at the cesura are usually possible.   In the fourth line we may ignore the cesura and see a simple anapestic substitution for an iamb.   In the penultimate line, similarly, we might scan a normal iamb in the fourth foot, creating a lyric cesura, followed by a final anapestic substitution.   But this would violate our principle of scansion, since a change in the modality of the line is more exceptional than a simple redundance before the cesura and a trochaic inversion after it.

The epic cesura, with its extra slack at the end of the first section, is analogous to a hypercatalexis at the end of a line. The second section, for its part, might begin with an extra slack, in a process similar to anacrusis, and we can call it an **anacrusis cesura**:

Iambic pentameter:

> Your hearts I'll stamp out with my horse's heels,
> And make a quagmire of your mingled brains.
> Convey me Salisbury into his tent,
> And then we'll try ‖ what these dastard Frenchmen dare.
>
> x   − | x   − | x   x   −|x   − | x   −
>   *anacrusis cesura*

In older manuscripts and books, commas were sometimes inserted to indicate the cesura.

In the Degrees of Stress (Modification)

We saw earlier a basic paradox in the meter-rhythm relationship—the meter must derive from the normal prose rhythms, yet, once established, it may dictate to some extent how the words ought to be *modified* in their pronunciation. It can require that a word or syllable carry two different values in two places in the line:

> I know when one is dead and when one lives.
> x   − | x   − |x   − | x   − | x −

The word "one" changes its status from stress to slack largely because the preceding word, "when," changes in the opposite direction. "When" changes because of the syllables that precede it in each case: "know" is strong, logically and syntactically, and therefore is most easily followed by a slack;

"and" is weak, thus calling for a strong pronunciation to follow it. The point is that all these relationships are conditioned by our desire to maintain an even alternation between stresses and slacks wherever possible. So the meter helps to modify the language of prose into the more stylized language of poetry. See how the stress pronunciation of the italicized words shifts in this passage:

Iambic pentameter couplets:

That, Virtue's ends from Vanity can raise,
Which seeks *no* int'rest, *nó* reward but praise;
And build *on* wants, and *ón* defects *of* mind,
The joy, the peace, the glory *óf* Mankind.

(The last line may be scanned with a concluding ionic.)

The English language has many monosyllabic words, most of which are capable of serving either as slack or as stress. We cannot say that any given syllable in itself carries primary or secondary or tertiary stress: it depends on how it contrasts with the syllables in its vicinity. Our desire for a contrasting alternation of stronger with weaker stresses is sufficiently demanding so that when three slacks come together we tend to promote the middle one; if three stresses, to demote the middle one. For example, the three syllables in the two words "uphill" and "walk" are all capable of strong stress. Yet when we put them together the middle syllable can be demoted:

walk uphill   uphill walk
— x̂ —   — x̂ —

We depend on personal judgment and sensitivity. Take the word "sensitivity" itself. We can see it as containing one significant stress:

sensitivity
x   x —x x

But the metrical pattern might attune us to one of the medial stresses in the word so that we promote it to metrical ictus:

> sensitivity
> $\hat{-}$ x—xx

Or if the meter is strong enough and demands it, we may want to promote both medials:

> sensitivity
> $\hat{-}$ x—x$\hat{-}$

Generally, then, promotion and demotion are modifications of the degree of stress required in normal prose speech. They are promotion and demotion *from* prose rhythms. Let us take a closer look at how they operate in actual metrical contexts.

Promotion

The iambic pentameter line often contains only four clear *rhythmic* stresses. We are then required to promote one syllable in order to get five *metrical* stresses:

> Much have I travelled in the realms of gold
> —   x |x — | x $\hat{-}$| x — |x —
>   ↑
>   *promotion*

or:

> Of Angels by Imperial summons call'd,
>
> Innumerable before th' Almighties Throne.
> x — |x $\hat{-}$| x — | x   —| x   —
>   ↑

Pentameters with only 3 strong prose stresses require 2 promotions:

Immútable, Immórtal, Ínfinite   *prose stresses*
x   −|x ⌢ |x   − |x − |x ⌢   *meter*

    ↑   ↑

or:

Unréspited, unpítied, unrepréevd
x   −| x⌢ |x −|x   ⌢ |x −

The promotion very often comes as the last syllable of the line, causing, as we have seen, a light ending:

Iambic pentameter:

And well deserving? Yet I know her for
      x   −   x ⌢

A spleeny Lutheran, and not wholesome to
        −   x   ⌢

Our cause, that she should lie i' the bosom of
       x − x   ⌢

Our hard-ruled King. Again, there is sprung up
        x   x   −   −   (or x⌢x̂⌢)

A heretic, an arch one, Cranmer, one
      −   x ⌢

Hath crawled in to the favor of the King.

That example is somewhat unusual, since light endings do not occur as frequently with monosyllabic words as with polysyllabic ones:

Iambic pentameter:

We do it wrong, being so majestical,
          x — x ⌒

To offer it the show of violence,
          —x ⌒

For it is as the air invulnerable,
          x — x ⌒

And our vain blows malicious mockery.
          — x ⌒

The poet may have light endings both at the end of the line and at the cesura:

Iambic pentameter:

Hard on our Lord's Ascension, it began

To be more sensible. A gentleman
     — x ⌒ ‖x — x ⌒

Demotion (Suppression)

What are we to do with this line, in the middle of some iambic pentameters?

Rocks, Caves, Lakes, Fens, Bogs, Dens, and shades of death.

Some metrists will assign several "spondaic substitutions" and move on. But we should not be so sophisticated that we overlook the obvious fact that the poet is clearly undertaking a very special excursion from the meter. We see immediately that the line is uncommon, but unless we try to scan it with our standard equipment we will have no basis for discussing its uncommonness. The question we need to ask when faced with such a line is not: How can we show that this line is in fact metrical? but rather: Can this line still *qualify* under the metrical demands when the poet has gone so obviously far from the meter? No one will deny that the line has eight clear and strong prose stresses. But we are not dealing with free verse, and the effectiveness of the metrical deviation here certainly depends on the way that the poet still obeys the metrical law, if only in theory, while ranging so far from it in spirit. Context is important here. In itself, the line may be considered an eight-stress accentual line. But it happens to occur in a poem of over ten thousand lines that gravitate around the iambic pentameter, usually containing ten syllables and five metrical stresses. In the light of this we ought to see whether it might not at least qualify for the norm.

We notice that the line contains exactly ten syllables, as the norm requires. The last four syllables fall clearly into two simple iambs, and this leaves six syllables problematical, six monosyllabic words in a row. We would like to give them six stresses but may not, since, having already distributed two stresses among the last four syllables, we have only three stresses left. The question now becomes: Can we in fact pronounce six monosyllabic nouns in a row with equal stress, or do we give a preferred emphasis? Some such preference may be reinforced by the context of the iambic pentameter norm, established over many lines, and in this case perhaps even in the fact that "fens" and "dens" rhyme (rhyme usually adding emphasis to a syllable), while "dens" alliterates with "death," which we know to be stressed. If we are willing to consider these two words as more heavily pronounced than their neighbors, we have assigned four of the metrical stresses that the norm requires. Moving toward the beginning of the line, we would probably choose to assign a stress to "caves," thus making a line, metrically speaking, of simple iambic pentameter, arrived at through the process of demoting three syllables:

Rocks, Caves, Lakes, Fens, Bogs, Dens, and shades of death.
x̂   — | x̂   — | x̂   — | x   — | x   —

If your pronunciation is sensitive to some other pattern of alternation of strong stresses with extra strong stresses, you may decide on some such other scansion, as:

Rocks, Caves, Lakes, Fens, Bogs, Dens, and shades of death.
—   x̂ | x̂   — | x̂   — | x   — | x —

If you cannot accept the idea that any of the first six syllables are weaker than any others, even under the pressure of the norm, you may want to decide that this line satisfies only the decasyllabic feature of the norm, or that the poet here breaks out of the norm entirely. For some reason, most of us allow demotion less willingly than we do promotion.

So we must sometimes decide whether to regard a passage of poetry as a free variation or as an example of extreme tension between rhythm and meter. Metrists who cannot believe that some stresses in such a line are in fact stronger than others, but who on the other hand do not want to believe that the poet has abandoned his meter, have sometimes resorted to a kind of compromise scansion called **hovering accent** or **distributed stress**. This is a scansion that establishes the required number of stresses without making a commitment as to exactly which syllables will carry them. When it is said that a stress is distributed over two syllables, what is meant is that the stress is made available to either of those syllables, with the understanding that either may take the role of metrical stress, leaving the other to be the slack. This adheres to metrical principles without making a final metrical decision. Distributed stress or hovering accent may be marked:

Rocks, Caves, Lakes, Fens, Bogs, Dens, and shades of death.
          | | | x   — | x —

The hovering accent is a convenient way of telling your reader that he can make his own choice without fear of disturbing the metrical norm:

Howl, howl, howl, howl! Oh, you are men of stones.
          | | —   x | x   — | x   —

These are unusual cases, examples of metrical acrobatics. More common are lines where the required demotion is not so puzzling:

Die not, poor Death, nor yet canst thou kill me.
x̂ – | x̂   – | x̂ –| x̂   x   – –
                        | x̂   –̂ | x̂ —

Or the third line of this passage:

Iambic pentameter:

My lord, our army is dispersed already.
Like youthful steers unyoked, they take their courses
East, west, north, south, or, like a school broke up,
Each hurries toward his home and sporting place.

And here is an example of how the poet pulls the prose rhythm against the meter with a good deal of demotion and then returns clearly to a strong iambic pentameter form:

Ore bog or steep, through strait, rough, dense, or rare,
x̂ – | x – | x̂   – | x̂   – | x –

With head, hands, wings, or feet pursues his way,
x – | x̂   – | x – | x — | x –

And swims or sinks, or wades, or creeps, or flyes.
x – | x – | x – | x – | x –

We must remember that a line's rhythm, and hence our decision as to whether to promote or demote syllables, depends on the contrast of a syllable with its neighbors. In the fourth line of the passage

Here whips on whips excite perpetual fears,

And mingled howlings vibrate on my ears;

Here nature's plagues abound, to fret and tease,

Snakes, scorpions, despots, lizards, centipedes
x̂   – | x – |x –|x – |x –̂

we are allowed five stresses, and the line is composed of five nouns. But it turns out, metrically, that the monosyllabic noun beginning the line must be demoted to slack while the trisyllabic one at the end is awarded two stresses, one of them through promotion.

Here is an example of the general rhythmic flexibility that can be achieved through a mixture of promotion, demotion, and trochaic, ionic, and anapestic substitutions in an iambic pentameter:

And there, there overhead, there, there, hung over
x   — | — x|x   — | x̂   — | x̂ — | x

Those thousands of white faces, those dazed eyes,
x   — |x   x   — — |x   x   —   —

There in the starless dark the poise, the hover,
—   x| x   —|x   — | x   — | x   —|x

There with vast wings across the canceled skies,
—   x | x̂   — | x — | x — |x   —

There in the sudden blackness the black pall
— x | x — |x   — | x   x   —   —

Of nothing, nothing, nothing—nothing at all.
x   — |x   — |x   — |x   — |x   x   —

In the Number of Syllables (Alteration)

Alteration is the changing of the length of a word by pronouncing it with more or fewer syllables than we ordinarily do. The problem here is that one man's compression of a word may be another's normal pronunciation, or that what seems to us exceptional may have been, in the poet's time, standard or common variation. So when we think of compression and extension as devices the author purposely uses to depart from his own normal pronunciation, we are sometimes using another convenient fiction. Most of the time, however, we take no special notice of alterations and simply allow the scansion to indicate any unusual pronunciations, such as "patience" in this four-stress context:

Since patience I must have perforce
x   − |x   − |x   − | x   −

I live and hope in patience
x − | x   − |x   −|x −

Compression (Apocopation, Elision)

Compression is a blanket term that we may use to cover any instance where we scan two syllables of our *ordinary* pronunciation as one *metrical* syllable. What actually happens in our pronunciation is extremely varied—we drop syllables, or slur them together with other syllables, or pronounce them quickly to take up the *time* of a single syllable, or perform any of the activities described by such terms as *contraction*, *amalgamation, suppression, shortening, coalition, omission, aphaeresis, smearing, slurring, gliding, eliding, apocopating, compression, jamming, syncope, synaeresis, synezesis, synechphonesis*, and *monosyllabification*. Great arguments are waged over the nature of the reader's vocal activity as he does these various things, but it will suffice us to regard compression as occurring wherever two syllables should be at least theoretically pronounced as one, for the sake of the meter.

This is another matter of choice: where one metrist will compress two adjoining slacks, another will render a trisyllabic substitution. It is probably best to prefer compression—itself at times a popular convention—to modal shift wherever it can be reasonably accepted.

For the sake of convenience we can subdivide metrical compressions into two categories: those where compression has already been performed in the printed text through the replacing of a syllable by an apostrophe, and those where both syllables still remain in the printed text, leaving us to decide for ourselves whether to reduce them to one. For the

typographically marked compression we can adopt the term
apocopation; for the other kind, the term **elision**.

So apocopation is, in effect, the announcement in the spelling and punctuation of the printed text that compression has
already taken place, either of unaccented prefixes of words
(e.g., *'bove* for *above*, *'cause* for *because*, *'longs* for *belongs*)
or, more loosely, of any missing syllables (e.g., *'tis* for *it is*,
flow'r for *flower*, *ev'ry* for *every*, *I'm* for *I am*, *wond'rous* for
wonderous):

> But I can tell you that of late this Duke

> Hath ta'en displeasure 'gainst his gentle niece.
> x   — | x — |x   — | x — | x —

One of the troublesome things about these apostrophes is
that they did not *always* indicate the dropping of a syllable.
Orthographic conventions change, and the apostrophe was
sometimes used merely to save time in copying or to indicate
that the missing syllable ought to be pronounced lightly; it
did not always mean that a syllable was to be compressed.
When, therefore, we are confronted with an apostrophe, we
should be ready to reinstate the missing syllable if, as happens
on rare occasions, the meter seems to require it:

> For we are far from flatt'ring our friend
> x   —|x   —| x   —|x — | x   —

(Reading a final anapest would render a four-stress line in a
pentameter context.)

On the other hand, an apostrophe may appear where no
syllable is lacking. This usually seems to be a signal that the
syllables surrounding the apostrophe are to be pronounced
quickly together so that they will count as a single syllable
metrically, or even that they should be elided into one:

> And yet, for any weightie, 'and great affaire
>
> x   — | x —| x — | x   — |x —

Here are two examples of apocopation. The first is striking because it reduces a girl's name from two syllables to one. The girl's name is Una:

Then forth he called that his daughter fayre,
x — | x —|x   — | x   — | x —

The fairest Un', his onely daughter dear.
x —|x   — | x —|x   — | x   —

(To preserve the metrical norm, the poet here declines to use even an epic cesura.) The second example is striking because it contains an apocopation immediately followed by an elision, to form the two stresses of an ionic foot:

What sense had I of her stol'n hours of lust?
x — | — x|x x —   — | x —

Elision is any method by which we regard two printed syllables as metrically one. This line is compressed from thirteen syllables to ten:

No, faith, she let it drop by negligence,

And, to the advantage, I being here took 't up.
—   x| x —| x —| x   — | x   —
        ↑   ↑   ↑
     elision   *elision*   *apocopation*

A normal iamb is a smoother possible way of starting this line, but the trochaic inversion is indicated by the logic and the punctuation. Moreover, it is a speech that calls for awkwardness of tongue.

In this case one word ("seven") is scanned, through elision, in three different ways:

Edward's seven sons, whereof thyself art one,

  –   x | x   – | x –| x – |x –

Were as seven vials of his sacred blood,

     – x | – x | –   x| x – |x   –

Or seven fair branches springing from one root.

     x   – | x   – | x   – |x   – |x   –

Here are more examples, to illustrate the variety attainable through elision:

Stiffly to stand on this and proudly approve

    –   x |x   – |x   –|x   – | x   –

Anguish and doubt and fear and sorrow and pain

   –   x |x   – | x – |x   –| x   –

Of Rainbows and Starrie Eyes. The Waters thus

   x   – | x   x   –   – | x –|x   –

Consider the following lines, in an iambic pentameter context:

Created hugest that swim th' Ocean stream

So he with difficulty and labour hard

Mov'd on, with difficulty and labour hee.

Certain disyllabic words, where the first syllable is long and the second short and where the two syllables become elided into one, are called **hypermonosyllables**. They are usually scanned as a single syllable but are available for disyllabic

scansion if the meter requires it. Common examples of hypermonosyllables are *power, shower, flower, bower, prayer, cruel,
being, dying, ever, evil,* etc. With such words the monosyllabic
value is often apocopated into *pow'r, pray'r, e'er,* etc.:

> For me kind Nature wakes her genial pow'r,
> Suckles each herb, and spreads out ev'ry flow'r.

Extension

Extension is the reverse of compression. Again, changes in
the language are involved, since many of our own pronunciations are compressions of older forms, such as *childeren,
bretheren, enterance, Engeland, shortely, juggeler, busyness,*
and *thorough.* So, by the term extension, we mean simply
the adding of a syllable to what *we* consider to be the standard
length of a word. Notice the various degrees of extension in
the lines:

> Became the accents of the valiant
> $-x\overset{\frown}{-}$

> All the sad spaces of oblivion
> $x\ -x\overset{\frown}{-}$

> And yet 'tis almost 'gainst my conscience
> $-\ \ x\overset{\frown}{-}$

> But Brutus says he was ambitious
> $x\ \ -x\overset{\frown}{-}$

> To woo a maid in way of marriage
> $-\ x\overset{\frown}{-}$

In these examples, the last syllable of each line is extended. It is also promoted to stress, creating a light ending. This is logical, since it was the need for one more stress that produced the extension in the first place.

The demand for extension can also be supported by rhyme, but even without that help, the sensitive iambic pentameter will indicate when we ought to extend and when not. More often than not, such extensions come at the end of the line:

> And think how such an apprehension
>   − x−
>
> May turn the tide of fearful faction,
>   − x−
>
> And breed a kind of question in our cause.
>   − x

Wherever it occurs, the extension is performed in service to the meter and may be put into effect one moment and not the next:

> Ne may love be compeld by maistery;   *maistery*
> −   x |−   x | x   − | x   −|x −
>
> For soone as maistery comes, sweet Love anone   *maistery*
>   x   − |x   −|x   − | x   − |x −

Here is a striking example, where the extension is signaled by the shift in spelling:

> That sayd, her rownd about she from her turnd,   *turnd*
> x̂   − | x̂   − |x −| x   − | x   −
>
> She turned her contrary to the sunne,   *turned*
> x   −| x   −| x   −|x ̂| x   −
>
> Thrise she her turnd contrary, and returnd   *turnd*
>   −   x | x   − |x   −|x ̂ |x −

All contrary, for she the right did shunne,
x   — | x— | x   — | x   — | x   —

And ever what she did was streight undonne.
x — |x   — | x   — | x   — | x —

(Note also the shift in the pronunciation of "contrary.") But
sometimes spelling is misleading for our modern ears:

Your daughter and her cousin much commend

The parts and graces of the wrestler.
— x—

In Substitution

Of other Feet

In the iambic pentameter the most common substitutions
for iambic feet are trochaic ones; next in popularity are the
ionics. This is significant because the trochee and the ionic
keep up the one-to-one ratio between stresses and slacks.
Anapests are much rarer because they are trisyllabic, creating
a modal shift from duples to triples. We do well, in our
scansion of iambics, to allow anapestic substitutions only
when we must, so that we can be more sensitive to the
difference between the stricter and the looser forms of the
iambic pentameter (those that exclude, and those that allow,
modal shift). A poem that maintains a strictly duple *meter*,
as we have seen, can still create the effect of triple *rhythm*
by combining iambs, trochees, and ionics:

When to the sessions of sweet, silent thought
—   x| x   — | x   x   —   —| x   —   *duple meter*
                                                                        (5 stresses,
                                                                        5 slacks)

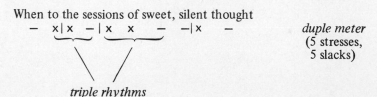

triple rhythms

Trochaic. The trochaic substitution among iambics is an
inversion. It occurs most often as the first foot of the line,
and next as the first foot after the cesura. If the trochee is
followed by a regular iamb, the *rhythm* created is the choriambic:

$$- x \mid x - \mid x - \mid x - \mid x -$$

$\uparrow$
choriambic rhythm

Here, the strong first syllable is a surprise. Since it disrupts
the iambic progression, we look for some return to normality.
This is achieved by the occurrence, following the first stress,
of two slacks instead of one.

When, however, the first unusual stress is followed by an
even alternation of slacks and stresses:

$$- x - x - x \ldots$$

we are put into temporary perplexity. Is this a truncated
line? (We may want to count the syllables.) Has the meter
itself changed from iambic to trochaic? Are we scanning
with the proper promotions and demotions, compressions
and extensions? When we encounter an unexpected stress in
the iambic pentameter line, we benefit from the habit of
quickly looking for a triple rhythm somewhere in that line.
When we find such a triple rhythm:

$$- x - x - x x - \ldots$$

it usually indicates that the iambics have returned to normal
and that all the feet up to that point were trochaic substitutions:

trochees   *iambs*

$$- x \mid - x \mid - x \mid x - \mid x -$$

recovery
(triple rhythm)

This return to normal meter, or **recovery**, involves a **compensation** in the meter. In strict iambics, the poet is expected to preserve the alternation of stresses and slacks. So we expect the appearance of two consecutive slacks to compensate for the appearance of two consecutive stresses elsewhere in the line. (The ionic foot is a paradigm of this kind of compensation.) In a normal trochaic substitution within the line, the two stresses appear first and are compensated by two slacks:

$$x - | - \quad x | x - | x - | x -$$

compensation

A trochaic inversion, in order to disrupt the rhythm successfully, will commonly begin with a particularly strong stress. It is therefore disconcerting when the stress of the trochee is so weak that it must be promoted, disconcerting because the entire metrical pattern will then be momentarily obscured:

The world is charged with the grandeur of God.
$$x \quad - | x \quad - | \quad \hat{\cdot} \quad x | - \quad x | x \quad -$$
$$\uparrow$$
promotion
at trochee

Here, "with" seems to be so much weaker than "charged" that we hesitate to allow it a stress until we discover that the following "the" is even weaker. Also disconcerting is the fact that the recovery is not achieved until the last foot. Taking this line by itself, our first scansion might be $|x -|x -|xx -|xx -|$, but the line happens to occur in a pentameter context. One other way to scan it would be by extending "charged" to two syllables, thereby creating an anapestic substitution at the end of the line:

The world is charged with the grandeur of God.
$$x \quad - | x \quad - | x \quad \hat{\cdot} \quad | x \quad - | x \quad x \quad -$$

A similar case where inversion and promotion combine to make a confusing conflict between the rhythm and meter occurs in the line:

$$x- \quad x- x \quad x \ - x \quad x \ -$$
Before thy fellows, ambitious to win
$$x- \ | \ x- |x \quad \overset{\frown}{-} \ | - x \ |x \ -$$

rhythm (4-stress)

meter   (5-foot)

When a trochaic inversion begins the second section of a line, the result is a cesura having stresses on both sides. This breaks up the rhythmic alternation and creates what has been called a **broken-backed line**:

$$x- \ | \ x- \ | \ x \overset{\|}{-}\underbrace{| \ -} x \ | \ x \ -$$

The effect at the cesura is the same as if the second section had merely been truncated. But the metrical concept of the entire line is different, since truncation is not followed by a recovery as a trochee is:

trochee

To be, or not to be—that is the question

$$x \ \ -|x \ \ -|x \ \ \overset{\|}{-}| \ \ - \ x|x \ \ \ \ -|x$$

broken-backed compensation recovery

Another interesting relationship between the trochee and the cesura is that the cesura may cut through the trochee, creating a **counter-cesural inversion**:

$$x- \ | \ x- \ | \underbrace{- \overset{\|}{}x} \ | \ x- \ | \ x -$$

trochee

as in:

Nor streit'ning Vale, nor Wood, nor Stream divides

Thir perfet ranks; for high above the ground

Thir march was, ‖and the passive Air upbore

x   — | —   x | x   —|x   —|x   —

counter-cesural inversion

(You may prefer a simpler |x —|x ‖ ⌐|x —|x —|x —|.)
    The trochaic inversion may occur in any of the five feet,
least frequently in the fifth. To find these trochees in one
line of iambic pentameter is rare, but on occasion we even
find five:

She sang beyond the genius of the sea.

The water never formed to mind or voice,

Like a body wholly body, fluttering.

—   x| — x| —   x| — x| —   x

(If you want to pronounce "fluttering" with three syllables,
you have a final trochee followed by a feminine ending.)

Ionic.   While the trochaic substitution creates a choriambic rhythm, the ionic substitution creates the familiar
cadence sometimes described as a pyrrhic followed by a
spondee.   The stresses involved are usually rather strong
because they need to overcome the iambic movement; they
appear all the stronger, therefore, when they follow a line
where promotion is necessary, as in this sample of iambic
tetrameter:

Yet it creates, transcending these,

Far other Worlds, and other Seas;

Annihilating all that's made
x −|x⁀|x − | x   −

To a green Thought in a green Shade.
 x x −   − |x x −   −

Here are lines where the ionic movement helps to bring together all three stresses in the second section:

And the wheel's kick and the wind's song‖and the
  x   x   −   − | x   x   −   − | x   x

    white sail's shaking,
    − − | − x

And a grey mist on the sea's face‖and a grey dawn breaking.
  x x − − |x x − − | x x − − | − x

Here is an extended passage where ionics and trochees share the job of creating triple rhythms while maintaining a duple metrical mode:

I sought a theme and sought for it in vain,
x − |x − | x   − | x ⁀|x −

I sought it daily for six weeks or so.
x − |x −|x x −   − |x −

Maybe at last, being but a broken man,
  − x|x − | x   −|x −|x   −

I must be satisfied with my heart, although
x − | x −| x   ⁀ | x − |x   −

Winter and summer till old age began
— x |x   — | x x — — | x —

My circus animals were all on show
x   — |x —|x ⌃̣ | x   — |x   —

A cluster of three stresses in a row is especially unusual in the iambic pentameter:

On the rich quilt sinks with becoming woe
x   x —   — |—   x | x — |x   —

(Or perhaps ⌣̇ x|— x̂|— x|x —|x —.)

The role of the ionic as a standard variation in iambic pentameter is an important one. Remembering that it counts metrically as two feet, we can formulate the relationship between it and the norm as:

$3(x -) + 1(xx - -) = 3$ feet $+ 2$ feet $= 5$ feet with iambic base.

Often, the ionic foot may be avoided and the scansion simplified in either of two ways, depending on the judgment of the metrist:
(1) When two stresses or two slacks appear consecutively, we may hear the second as slightly stronger than the first. In that case we can use the contrast in the *relative* degrees of stress as the basis for scansion:

In confus'd march
x   x   —   —

may be scanned: x   ⌣̇ | x̂   —

on the basis that "con" is stronger than "In," and "march" stronger than "fus'd."   In the word "confus'd," to be sure, the second syllable is clearly stronger than the first. But these two syllables fall into separate iambs and may be contrasted merely to the other syllables in their own feet. In the phrase "the supreme King," likewise, "su" and "King" can be heard as relatively stronger than "the" and "preme," again forming two iambs instead of one ionic.

(2) **Recession of accent** is the phenomenon where a disyllabic adverb or adjective stressed on the second syllable ("confús'd," "supréme"), when followed by a noun or verb stressed on the first syllable ("march," "King"), shifts its accent backward so that two strong stresses will not have to come together:

confus'd march   supreme King

x —   —   x —   —

recession of accent → — x   —   — x   —

Again, if you think that the pronunciation of this **recessional stress-shift** sounds too artificial, or if you do not know the historically normal pronunciation, you may prefer to scan the phrase with the ionic substitution. Pronunciations do change. The best rule is to remain flexible, to scan words in the way that seems most reasonable at the moment.

There may also be some use in the idea of a **descending (falling) ionic** foot, also called the **greater ionic**:

Still through the dusk of dead, blank-legended

—   x | x — |x — | —   — x x

although here again it can be avoided:

blank-legended

x̂   —|x   ᷄

Anapestic. The more liberal examples of foot-meters allow modal shift metrically as well as rhythmically, and this is almost always done with the anapest.

The iambic norm has ten syllables. An anapestic substitution normally brings it to eleven, so three-elevenths of the line is supposedly part of an anapestic foot. The anapest therefore usually will fall at the beginning or end of a line, or before or after the cesura, and at any of these four points the extra syllable can be accounted for extrametrically. For example:

> A pig with a pasty face, so I had said,
> x −| x　x −|x −　| x−| x　−　　　　　　　　*anapest*

> Squealing for cookies, kinned by poor pretense
> −x　| x　− | x　　−　　| x　−　|　x−

> With a noble house. But the little man quite dead,
> x　x −| x −　　| x　x −| x　− | x̂　　−　　　　*anapests*

> I see the forbears' antique lineaments.
> x −　| x −| x　　−|x　　−| x　⌒

The three anapests here could be disposed of by rules that preserve the duple modality of the traditional iambic pentameter. The first line might be taken as a simple anacrusis followed by a trochaic inversion: x|− x|x −|x −|. . . . The third line could be taken as having one anacrusis to start the line and another, after the cesura, to start the second section. So we have a choice between a simpler scansion (using anapestic substitutions) or a more complicated one that is able to indicate how the variations come only at the beginning or the break of a line.

In the example below, we can take the second line as containing an ionic followed by an anapest:

> It looked as if a night of dark intent

> Was coming, and not only a night, an age
> x　− |x　x　− −|x x　− | x　−

or merely an epic cesura:

> Was coming,‖and not only a night, an age.
> x　− | (x)　x　−|− x|x　− | x　−

Our decisions in such cases will be influenced by the degree of strictness or permissiveness that the context indicates. Here is one passage of fairly strict iambic pentameter where the anapestic substitutions are clear:

If thou dost nod, thou break'st thy instrument,

I'll take it from thee, and, good boy, good night.

Let me see, let me see, is not the leaf turned down
x   x − | x   x   −

Of other Lines

Alexandrines. One of the most popular variations to the length of the pentameter is a line of six stresses and usually twelve syllables, called the iambic hexameter or **alexandrine**:

Iambic pentameter:

When I was dry with rage and éxtreme toil,

Breathless and faint, leaning upon my sword,

Came there a certain lord,ǁneat, and trimly dressed,
−   x | x − |x   − | ()− | x   − |x   −   *alexandrine*

Fresh as a bridegroom, and his chin new-reaped

Showed like a stubble land at harvest home.

The alexandrine variation appears also in rhymed pentameters:

But short shall be his Reign: his rigid Yoke
And Tyrant Pow'r will puny Sects provoke;
And Frogs and Toads, and all the Tadpole Train
Will croak to Heav'n for help, from this devouring Crane.   *alex.*

We are sometimes faced with a choice, when traditional pentameters shift ambiguously into what can be either alexandrines or loose accentual five-stress lines:

> Held up by standards wrought with fruited vines
> From which a golden Cupidon peeped out
> (Another hid his eyes behind his wing)

> Dóubled the flámes of sévenbranched cándelábra   *5-stress*
> — x | x — |x —|x — | x — | x— | x   *alexandrine*

Some poets use the alexandrine as a standard variation in iambic pentameter while others exclude it rigidly. The alexandrine is particularly common in poetic drama. We often find a three-foot section concluding one speech and another three-footer beginning the next, the rhythmical echo creating a bridge between speakers:

> *MACBETH.* Send out moe horses, skirr the country round,
> Hang those that talk of fear. Give me mine armor.
> How dóes your pátient, Dóctor?
>   } *alexandrine*
> *DOCTOR.*   Nót so síck, my lórd, }
> As she is troubled with thick-coming fancies
> That kéep her fróm her rést.
>   } *pentameter*
> *MACBETH.*   Cúre her of thát. }
> Canst thou not minister to a mind diseased,
> Pluck from the memory a rooted sorrow

The seven-foot iambic line, or **septenary**, is also sometimes used to vary the pentameter:

> Almighty Crowd, thou shorten'st all dispute;
> Pow'r is thy Essence; Wit thy Attribute!
> Nor Faith nor Reason make thee at a stay,
> Thou leapst o'r all eternal truths, in thy *Pindarique*
>   way!   *septenary*

Dimeters. The pentameter is also varied by lines of four or three feet, but most usual, after the alexandrine, is the **dimeter variation** of two feet. It is often used in extended passages to break the blocklike effect or to signal paragraph structure:

> From me, whose love was of that dignity
> That it went hand in hand even with the vow
> I made to her in marriage, and to decline
> Upon a wretch whose natural gifts were poor
> To those of mine!   *dimeter*
> But virtue, as it never will be moved,
> Though lewdness court it in a shape of Heaven,
> So Lust, though to a radiant angel linked,
> Will sate itself in a celestial bed,
> And prey on garbage.   *dimeter*
> But soft! Methinks I scent the morning air

The more relaxed types of iambic pentameter will seem to gravitate around a norm rather than follow it. Here is an example with unrhymed phrases:

Iambic pentameter with variant lines:

> That huge long train of fawning followers,
> That swept a furlong after me.   *tetrameter*
> 'Tis true I am alone;   *trimeter*
> So was the godhead, ere he made the world
> And better served himself than served by nature.
> And yet I have a soul   *trimeter*
> Above this humble fate. I could command,
> Love to do good, give largely to true merit,
> All that a king should do; but though these are not
> My province, I have scene enough within
> To exercise my virtue.   *trimeter*

Amphibious Sections. We have seen that, in drama, a speech will often conclude with a fragment of a line that is completed by another speaker. Sometimes, however, in a special use of line sections in iambic pentameter, a section appears between *two* partial lines and serves to complete both of them, filling out the metrical movement in both directions. This is an **amphibious section**, diagramed as Section B, below:

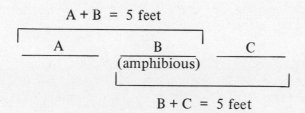

A + B = 5 feet

A   B   C
         (amphibious)

B + C = 5 feet

Here is an example where the amphibious section is trimeter, surrounded by dimeter sections:

MACDUFF.	What, all my pretty chickens and their dam	5
	At one fell swoop?	2
MALCOLM.	Dispute it like a man.	3
MACDUFF.	I shall do so,	2
	But I must also feel it as a man.	5

And here is a dimeter surrounded by trimeters:

CLAUDIO.	The weariest and most loathèd worldly life	5
	That age, ache, penury, and imprisonment	5
	Can lay on nature is a paradise	5
	To what we fear of death.	3
ISABELLA.	Alas, alas!	2
CLAUDIO.	Sweet sister, let me live.	3
	What sin you do to save a brother's life	5

In poetic drama especially, speeches may begin or end with short phrases (*alas, farewell, attend me, good my lord, come on,* etc.) that are sometimes to be regarded as extrametrical and are not to be counted in the scansion. If we wanted to, we could in the above example disregard "Alas, alas!" and "Sweet sister" as extrametrical, thereby rendering "To what we fear of death. Let me live" as a standard pentameter with truncated cesura. Commonly in drama, a change of speakers involves additional feet to the line, deficiency of feet, cata-lexes, truncations, and other cesural variations, line fragments, and amphibious sections.

SUMMARY–FOOT-VERSE SCANSION

In the scansion of foot-verse, our adherence to a proper order of business may be summarized in something like the following way:

(1) Preserve the definition of the foot as containing one stress exactly. (If it becomes inconvenient to maintain this definition, a foot-verse scansion will probably be pointless.)

(2) Determine how far the pronunciation may be reasonably altered to satisfy the requirements of the meter, through such processes as promotion, demotion, compression, and exten-sion.

(3) Determine what special addition or subtraction of slacks needs to be allowed at the end of the line, at the beginning, and at the cesura.

(4) Where foot substitution becomes necessary, preserve the modality if possible. Try to preserve the stress-slack ratio given in the norm. Prefer previously-used substitute feet to new ones.

(5) Keep variant lines as similar to the norm as possible.

It is important to remember that the goal of scansion is not flatly to label every syllable of a poem. Scansion, especially of foot-verse, is a convenient shorthand for communicating to others, and noting for ourselves, the general tendencies or laws that the poetic rhythms seem to create, and the many ways by which those rhythms seem also to escape the metrical rule. Sometimes we scan poetry simply to "check it out," to make sure that an ostensibly wild line is in fact within the poet's self-adopted rules and that the poet still has his materials under control. At other times we may scan in order to apprehend more directly the poet's technical imagination, as for example where he counterpoints triple rhythms with duple meters. This continual conflict between the natural rhythms of a language and the meter of the same language when stylized into poetry forms the basis for scansion.

So in order to scan poetry, we must learn to "listen" to rhythms, but we must also take care not to be misguided into hearing only the rhythm and ignoring the meter. Here, for example, are four lines, each having exactly ten syllables:

1 All the king's horses and all the king's men

2 Couldn't put Humpty together again

3 Getting and spending, we lay waste our pow'rs

4 When to the sessions of sweet, silent thought

In lines 1 and 2 we must hear that the controlling norm is one of four strong stresses to the line. We must also hear that lines 3 and 4 are more ambiguous. That ambiguity, together with our knowledge of larger context, should lead us to scan lines 3 and 4 as iambic pentameter (with standard substitutions). The key syllables are "waste" in line 3 and "si" in line 4: they could be demoted to slack, but a metrical field of pentameters will cause us to stress them.

No matter how well we learn to identify the standard patterns and all their variations, we must always be prepared to encounter some metrical activity we have not seen before. The poet is not obligated to follow rules, although his normal adherence to them makes his departures from them more significant. As metrists we can formulate rules and exceptions only to a certain point. It is not for us to say that the poet must not go beyond that point. We simply realize that if the poet carries us beyond it we will have to think in terms of special handling. The next four chapters deal with poetry that is awkward and sometimes impossible to scan with the apparatus of foot-verse. They suggest other metrical systems that can more economically and clearly describe other ways of organizing poetic rhythms.

CHAPTER III

SIMPLE STRESS-VERSE

From the intricacies of foot-verse we move now to a very simple form. In a way, stress-verse amounts to an entirely different philosophy of meter. Here the main interest is in having the proper number of stresses in each line. The slacks are not important metrically, however vital they may be to the actual rhythmic effects. They become a general background for the stresses and are not incorporated into the scansion.

When we are faced with a specific poem, it is not always easy to decide whether to scan it as foot-verse or as stress-verse. The boundary between the two types is not one of kind but of degree, even though they are radically different at their extremes. One often shades into the other: a loose iambic pentameter can be read as a moderately regular five-stress line. It sometimes becomes a matter of choosing between a precise, complicated description and a general, economical one.

Stress-verse is most clearly exemplified in poems where the number of stresses is fixed while the number of slacks per line varies freely. Because its stresses are not compelled to come at any fixed position in the line (in the iambic pentameter they would normally fall on syllables 2, 4, 6, 8, and 10), stress-verse is said to have a **roving accent**. This gives it a wide range of rhythmic possibilities and allows it to shift from formal regularity to free colloquial rhythms without ever losing metrical control, which is maintained so long as the main *markers* (the stresses, also called **supports** or **points**) are clearly present. Its construction, once the main supports are established, allows the spaces between them to be used for free ornamentation.

Stress-verse, then, as compared with foot-verse, has less *metrical* sensitivity to variation but greater *rhythmic* scope. We can see the general difference between the two forms if we compare some of the iambic pentameters in the previous chapter with this passage of five-stress verse:

5-stress (5s):

When mén were áll asléep the snów came flýing,
In lárge white flákes fálling on the cíty brówn,
Stéalthily and perpétually séttling and lóosely lýing,
    Húshing the látest tráffic of the drówsy tówn;
  Déadening, múffling, stífling its múrmurs fáiling;
Lázily and incéssantly flóating dówn and dówn:
    Sílently sífting and véiling róad, roof and ráiling;
Híding dífference, máking unévenness éven,
Into ángles and crévices sóftly drífting and sáiling.

Two important differences between this and the iambic pentameter are that stress-verse uses far less promotion and also permits three slacks to come consecutively. The iambics would usually promote one of those three slacks.

The most common stress-verse is the four-stress. It is capable of considerable jerkiness and roughness:

4-stress (4s):

I have héard that hystérical wómen sáy
They are síck of the pálette and fíddle-bów,
Of póets thát are álways gáy,
For éverybody knóws or élse should knów
Thát if nóthing drástic is dóne
Áeroplane and Zéppelin will cóme óut,
Pítch like King Bílly bómb-balls ín
Untíl the tówn lie béaten flát.

(The third and fifth lines require promotion or may be taken as 3s variations. "Should" in line 4 has high pitch but demoted stress.)

Much less common is the 2s norm, which shades into 3s for those who do not care to allow a good deal of demotion:

2/3-stress:

> Gíb, I sắy, our cát
> Wórrowëd hĕr on thát
> Whích I lóved bést.
> It cánnot bĕ expréssed—
> My sórrowful héavinĕss,
> But áll withŏut redréss;
> Fŏr withín that stóund,
> Half slúmb'ring, ĭn a swóund,
> I féll down tŏ the gróund.

(These lines seem to consist of two stronger and one weaker stress, with the weaker usually coming at the center. We could leave the meter unresolved by scanning it |— x ˰ x —|, with optional anacrusis.)

This ambiguity in the number of accents is another of the distinctive features of stress-verse, especially when it hovers between a 4s and a 5s norm. An **indeterminate** or **optional norm** may be the only "predictable" element in such cases:

4/5-stress:

```
      1           2         3     4
   Whan that Aprille with his shoures soote
         1     2   3      4      5


      1           2          3            4
   The droghte of March hath perced to the roote,
         1           2         3    4    5


      1             2        3    4
   And bathed every veyne in swich licour
      1      2    3         4    5


   1          2        3          4
   Of which vertu engendred is the flour.
   1         2        3     4    5
```

Here is a case where an ambiguous couplet modulates from a preferred five-stress to a preferred four-stress:

4/5-stress:

<pre>
     1   2   3   4
For had his wesand bene a little widder,   pref. 5s
     1   2   3   4   5
</pre>

<pre>
     1   2   3   4
He would have devoured both hidder and shidder.   pref. 4s
     1   2   3   4   5
</pre>

Sometimes even the preference is ambiguous:

4/5-stress:

> Cáptain Cárpenter róse up în his príme
> Pút on his pístols ând went ríding óut
> But hád got wéllnigh nówhere ât that tíme
> Tíll he fell ín with ládies în a róut.

Since the difference between stress-verse and foot-verse involves the predictability of slacks, a poet may shift from foot-verse to stress-verse by radically altering the number of slacks, either using more than the norm permits or else removing them:

Iambic pentameter———→5-stress:

> What art thou that usurp'st this time of night,   *IP*
> x – | x   –|x – | x – |x –

> Together with that fair and warlike form   „
> x –| x – | x – |x   –|x –

> In which the majesty of buried Denmark   „
> x   – | x –|x –|x – |x   –| x

> Did sometimes march? By Heaven I charge thee, speak!   „
>
> x – |x   – | x – |x – | x   –

It is offended. See, it stalks away!   *IP*
x −|x −| x   − |x   − |x −

Stay! Speak, speak! I charge thee, speak!   *5-stress*
1   2   3   4   5

The mingling of iambic pentameters—or even five-stress
lines—with stress-verse of other lengths is rather unusual and
worth noting:

I can see the breezy dome of groves,	4
The shadows of Deering's Woods;	3
And the friendships old and the early loves	4
Come back with a Sabbath sound, as of doves	4
In quiet neighborhoods.	3
And the verse of that sweet old song,	3
It flutters and murmurs still:	3
"A boy's will is the wind's will,	4
And the thóughts of yóuth are lóng, lóng thóughts."	5

3–3–5–3s:

Í have desíred to gó
    Where spríngs nót fáil,
To fíelds where flíes no shárp and síded háil
    And a féw lílies blów.

(Some ambiguity between 3s and 2s lines.)

3–5–5–3s (or 4–4–5–3s):

Béautifúlly Jánet slépt
Tíll it was déeply mórning. She wóke thén
And thóught abóut her dáinty-féathered hén,
To sée how ít had képt.

Here is an example of carefully mixed line-lengths in very regular iambics, varied only by trochaic inversions:

Get up, get up for shame, the blooming morn   5
Upon her wings presents the god unshorn.   5
   See how Aurora throws her fair   4
   Fresh-quilted colors through the air;   4
   Get up, sweet slug-a-bed, and see   4
   The dew bespangling herb and tree.   4
Each flower has wept and bowèd toward the east   5
Above an hour since, yet you not dressed.   5

But at other times the mixture of lines may be ambiguous, the shifting norm creating a sense of indeterminacy:

Áfter the tórchlight réd on swéaty fáces   5
Áfter the frósty sílence in the gárdens   5 (4)
Áfter the ágony in stóny pláces   4 (5)
The shóuting ánd the crýing   3 (2)
Príson and pálace ánd revérberátion   4 (3) (5)
Of thúnder of spríng óver dístant móuntains   4 (5)
Hé who was líving is nów déad   4
Wé who were líving are nów dýing   4
Wíth a líttle pátience   2 (3)

   Hére is no wáter but ónly róck   4
Róck and no wáter ánd the sándy róad   4 (5)
The róad wínding abóve amóng the móuntains   5
Whích are móuntains of róck withóut wáter   4 (3) (5)
Íf there were wáter wé should stóp and drínk   5 (4)
Amóngst the róck one cánnot stóp or thínk   5
Swéat is drý and féet are ín the sánd   5 (4)
Íf there were ónly wáter amóngst the róck   5

The peculiar effect of mixing stress-verse and foot-verse in this way is that the reader finds himself having to adjust his bearings, at one moment reading to get a sense of the "beat" of the line and at the next attuning himself to the interplay of slacks and stresses. He must shift his interest from rhythmic accents to metrical feet.

One of the main characteristics of stress-verse is that it establishes firmly a given stress-count in the line (most commonly four) and then demands a good deal of demotion. This creates a hardy, rough, sometimes jagged, but very active and energetic rhythm. It is in such cases that stress-verse is particularly felt to have a character of its own:

4-stress:

Stóp all the clócks, cút off the télephone,
Prevént the dog from bárking with a júicy bóne,
Sílence the piános and with múffled drúm
Bríng out the cóffin, lét the mourners cóme.
. . . .
He was my Nórth, my Sóuth, my Eást and Wést,
My wórking wéek and my Súnday rést,
My nóon, my mídnight, my tálk, my sóng;
I thóught that lóve would last for éver: I was wróng.

CHAPTER IV
STRESS-VERSE: THE NATIVE METERS

The "simple" stress-verse of the previous chapter involves a scansion that has little more to fix on than the counting of the number of stresses in the line. But there is a more rigid subtype of stress-verse, the native meters. Here the "markers" are still stresses rather than the syllable-stress combinations called feet. But now other elements also come into play, the cesura and, as will be discussèd, the pause. Though the line is still free to mix duple and triple rhythms, the number and the position of the stresses regarding the cesura are more strictly prescribed. The stresses (or their equivalents) are now arranged in multiples of two, and the distinction between primary stresses and secondary stresses becomes important. The native meters, in short, are specialized forms of stress-verse.

There are two main kinds of native meter: the Old Native Meter, no longer a standard form in English and commonly referred to as the Anglo-Saxon Alliterative Verse, and the Folk Meter that persists to our own time and is known in various guises such as "ballad meter" or "the meter of the hymnal." Whether or not the folk meters and the alliterative verse are historically related we cannot tell for certain. But they share a number of important characteristics, and a brief, broad look at the alliterative form can serve as a good introduction to the folk meters.

ANGLO-SAXON ALLITERATIVE VERSE

The basic metrical feature of the alliterative line is four strong stresses:

— — — —

The slacks vary a good deal and need not be included in the metrical scheme. Their omission does not mean that they are unimportant to the total effect. They are of course indispensable rhythmically, and it is only in contrast to them that we determine the stresses in the first place. But they do not appear consistently enough to generalize about or predictably enough to be useful in the scansion. The spaces between stresses can be occupied by two syllables, or one, or sometimes three, or sometimes none at all. If we were to include slacks in our scansion they might fall into such patterns as

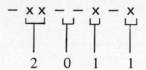

2   0   1   1   *consecutive slacks*

which obscures rather than clarifies the basic structure of four strong stresses.

In the alliterative verse, the cesura, a logical break, is *fixed* at the center of the line, dividing the first two stresses from the last two:

– – ‖ – –

The alliterative line is thus broken into half-lines or **hemistichs**, each hemistich usually totalling from four to eight syllables but having only two primary stresses. The two hemistichs combine into the **full-line**:

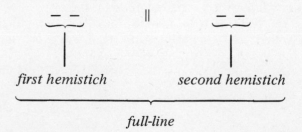

first hemistich   *second hemistich*

full-line

The distinctive feature of this metrical form is its **alliteration**. The informal meaning of the term is that two or more words in a passage begin with the same consonant. The formal requirements of alliteration, however, are that *three* (sometimes two) of the four stresses in each line fall on words beginning with the same consonant (or occasionally vowel). The third stress (the first one of the second hemistich) is called the **rhyme-giver** and always carries one of the alliterated consonants, while the last stress never does. Thus the alliterated consonant usually appears in the first three stresses, though it may be missing from the second or, less commonly, from the first. An alliterated line, where K represents a repeated consonant, can be symbolized:

$$(\underline{K}) \quad (\underline{K}) \quad \Big\| \quad \underline{K}$$
$$- \qquad - \quad \Big\| \quad - \quad -$$

In books, the alliterative line frequently appears with a colon (:), or with a space dividing the hemistichs:

Wæs sē grimma gǣst   Grendel hāten,

mǣre mearcstapa,   sē þe mōras hēold,

fen ond fæsten;   fīfelcynnes eard

wonsǣlī wer   weardode hwīle.

In time the alliterative verse became more flexible than the above requirements suggest and was used with more variations. Some of the hemistichs appeared with three stresses, to produce *lengthened lines*; the fourth stress was sometimes allowed to alliterate; the full-line would sometimes have two pairs of alliterations rather than one triple; and there was more ambiguity as to the placing of stresses. Some of these effects have been attempted in modern translations of Old English poems:

1 Bitter breast-cares have I abided,
    −   −   ‖   − −

2 Known on my keel many a care's hold,
    −   − ‖ −   −

3 And dire sea-surge, and there I oft spent
   —   —   ‖   —   —

4 Narrow nightwatch nigh the ship's head
   —   —   ‖ —   —

5 While she tossed close to cliffs. Coldly afflicted,
   (–)   (–)   —   — ‖ —   —

6 My feet were by frost benumbed.
   —   —   —   ‖

This passage contains a repetition of stressed vowels (I, bided) as well as of consonants (bitter, breast, bided). Line 2 allows a connection between the k-letter in "known" and "keel" on the basis of sight, not sound, while the k-sound is picked up in the second hemistich by the c of "care's." In line 5 we have four k-sounds, all produced by the letter c, but each of the c's is also in some way linked to the l-sound: in the first two stresses they come together in cl, but in the third stress they are separated, through the process of **augmentation,** by the o of "cold." In the fourth stress the k-sound does not begin the stressed syllable; the c and l combination is not only augmented but reversed, in "afflicted." Technically, this line has only a three-part alliteration, the first three stresses coming at "close," "cliffs," and "cold," while the fourth stress comes at "lic." The two hemistichs are further connected by the close similarities in the sound clusters that end them:

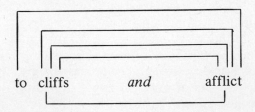

to cliffs   *and*   afflict

Here, the organizing features consist of sound-repetitions more than of rhythms and are not strictly involved with meter.

Note that the Anglo-Saxon four-stress line, especially in the way that it breaks into hemistichs, provides a framework upon which many kinds of effects can be built. Another sample of modernized alliterative verse follows:

> An axe angles
> > from my neighbor's ashcan;
> It is hell's handiwork
> > the wood not hickory,
> The flow of the grain
> > not faithfully followed.
> The shivered shaft
> > rises from a shellheap
> Of plastic playthings,
> > paper plates,
> And the sheer shards
> > of shattered tumblers
> That were not annealed
> > for the time needful.

FOLK METERS: GENERAL CHARACTERISTICS

Folk Meter shares some features with the Anglo-Saxon Alliterative Verse: the regularity or irregularity in the number of slacks does not affect the basic structure; the line contains a fixed cesura that divides it metrically in half; and the full-line is best understood as consisting of two half-lines or hemistichs. It also has some features of its own: it is usually rhymed; it more sensitively distinguishes between primary and secondary stresses, which tend to alternate with each other; the number of secondary stresses may vary, while the number of primary stresses per line is fixed at four; and the hemistichs can be of unequal length, creating flexibility of line-lengths and stanza-patterns.

Poems in Folk Meter are usually printed with the full-line *broken* into hemistichs, the second hemistich printed beneath the first and often indented. This means that, for a Folk Meter poem, what stands in the printed text as a quatrain (four-line stanza) can be regarded *structurally* as a couplet (two-line stanza).

The major forms of Folk Meter are discussed below.

LONG MEASURE, LONG METER (LM)

This is the simplest in structure and also the easiest to begin with, since all the others may be thought of as derivations from it. The term **Long Measure**, frequently abbreviated LM, originally referred to a line of 16 *syllables*, 8 slacks alternating with 8 stresses. But the line lends itself to scansion as *stress*-verse, with the distinctive pattern:

LM: $-$ $-$ $-$ $-$ $\parallel$ $-$ $-$ $-$ $-$

which is exactly twice as long as the alliterative line. When the LM line is broken and printed in hemistichs, it scans:

$-$ $-$ $-$ $-\parallel$

$-$ $-$ $-$ $-$

Notice the alternation of primary with secondary stresses in each hemistich:

	rhyme	stresses hemistich	full-line
Our king he has a secret to tell,	x	4	
And ay well keepit it must be:	a	4	8
The English lords are coming down	x	4	
To dance and win the victory.	a	4	8

Diagramed in full-lines, the stanza makes the pattern:

$$\textit{rhyme} \quad \textit{total stresses}$$

$$\breve{\;}' \;\; \breve{\;}' \;\; \breve{\;}' \;\; \breve{\;}' \;\; \| \;\; \breve{\;}' \;\; \breve{\;}' \;\; \breve{\;}' \;\; \breve{\;}' \qquad a \qquad 8$$

$$\breve{\;}' \;\; \breve{\;}' \;\; \breve{\;}' \;\; \breve{\;}' \;\; \| \;\; \breve{\;}' \;\; \breve{\;}' \;\; \breve{\;}' \;\; \breve{\;}' \qquad a \qquad 8$$

making one Folk Meter couplet. The distinction between primary and secondary stresses gives an indication of how the line might be performed and does not need to be included in the scansion. In hemistichs of four stresses, assigning of primary and secondary stresses may be only a matter of preference. Either:

> O where ha you been, Lord Randal, my son?

or:

> O whére ha you béen, Lord Randal, my son?

or:

preserves all the essential requirements of the hemistich. The important thing is that we preserve the proper number of stresses and the sense of alternation of primaries and secondaries—as far as possible. In some poems the alternation is weak or absent, and the number of stresses may be ambiguous.

The following selections illustrate the variety of effect possible to Long Measure.

Thén they 'r cómd on to Hútton Háll,	4 ⎫
They ráde that próper pláce abőut;	4 ⎭ 8
But the láird he wás the wíser mán,	4 ⎫
For hé had léft nae géar withőut.	4 ⎭ 8

(In the third line you may give a stress either to "he" or to "was.")

Náy, were thy són as góod as míne,   4

And óf some bóoks he cóuld but réad,   4

With swórd and búckler bý his síde,   4

To sée how hé could sáve his héad,   4

They míght have been cálld twó bold bréthren
Where éver théy did gó or ríde;
They míght have been cálld twó bold bréthren,
They míght have cráckd the Bórdersíde.

Come, sóund up your trúmpet and béat up your drúms,
And lét's go to séa with a váliant good chéer,
In séarch of a míghty vast návy of shíps,
The líke has not béen for these fífty long yéar.

(Notice the regularity of the slacks.)

The kíng was cúmand thro Cádden fórd,
And fíftene thóusand mén was hé;
They sáw the fórest thém befóre,
They thóught it áwsom fór to sée.

(Here the slacks create an almost completely regular duple rhythm.)

Ríde a cockhórse to Bánbury Cróss,   4
To sée a fine lády ón a white hórse,   4
With ríngs on her fíngers,   2 ⎫
And bélls on her tóes,   2 ⎬ 4
Shé shall have músic wheréver she góes.   4

(The third hemistich is broken into quarter-lines.)

Óh that I wére whére I wóuld be,
Thén would I bé whére I ám not;
But whére I ám thére I múst be,
And whére I wóuld be Í can nót.

———————

Humpty Dumpty sat on a wall,
Humpty Dumpty had a great fall.
   All the king's horses,
    And all the king's men,
Couldn't put Humpty together again.

———————

The modest Rose puts forth a thorn:
The humble Sheep, a threatning horn:
While the Lilly white, shall in Love delight
Nor a thorn nor a threat stain her beauty bright.

(Notice how the slacks are distributed.)

———————

How the Chimney-sweeper's cry
Every black'ning Church appalls;
And the hapless Soldier's sigh
Runs in blood down Palace walls.

———————

And ón that chéek, and ó'er that brów,   4
   So soft, so calm, yet eloquent,   4
The smiles that win, the tints that glow,   4
   But tell of days in goodness spent,   4
A mind at peace with all below,   4
   A heart whose love is innocent!   4

(This is a LM *triplet*, made of three full-lines.)

———————

Cómrades, léave me hére a líttle, whíle as yét 'tis éarly mórn;   8
Leave me here, and when you want me, sound upon the
   bugle-horn.   8

'Tis the place, and all around it, as of old, the curlews call,
Dreary gleams about the moorland flying over Locksley Hall.

(Two LM couplets, printed in full-lines.   Notice the even
rhythm, the perfect syllable-count, the cesuras, and the
rhymes.)

Sáfe in their álabáster chámbers,
Untouched by morning and untouched by noon,
Sleep the meek members of the resurrection,
Rafter of satin, and roof of stone.

Hé will téll me what Péter prómised,
And I, for wonder at his woe,
I shall forget the drop of anguish
That scalds me now, that scalds me now.

But one pale woman all alone,
   The dáylight kíssing her wán háir,
   Loitered beneath the gas lamps' flare,
With lips of flame and heart of stone.

What néed you, béing cóme to sénse,
But fúmble ín a gréasy tíll
And ádd the hálfpence tó the pénce
And práyer to shívering práyer, untíl
You have dríed the márrow fróm the bóne?
For men were born to pray and save:
Romantic Ireland's dead and gone,
It's with O'Leary in the grave.

(Two LM couplets. They are fused into a single LM quatrain because the fourth hemistich runs over into the fifth without any sense of stopping at the end; it is the only line-ending that runs on so quickly.)

Dónne, I suppóse, was súch anóther
Who fóund no súbstitúte for sénse,
To séize and clútch and pénetráte;
Éxpert beyónd expériénce.

The host with someone indistinct
Converses at the door apart,
The nightingales are singing near
The Convent of the Sacred Heart.

---

septembering arms of year extend
less humbly wealth to foe and friend
than he to foolish and to wise
óffered imméasuráble ís

---

stars rain sun moon
(and only the snow can begin to explain
how children are apt to forget to remember
with úp so flóating mány bells dówn)

"O where are you going?" said reader to rider,
"That valley is fatal when furnaces burn,
Yonder's the midden whose odours will madden,
That gap is the grave where the tall return."

Edgar Degas purchased once
A fine El Greco, which he kept
Against the wall beside his bed
To hang his pants on while he slept.

Ínfant, ít is enóugh in lífe
To spéak of whát you sée. But wáit
Until síght wákens the sléepy éye
And pierces the physical fix of things.

COMMON MEASURE, COMMON METER (CM)

Common Measure is found in hymns, nursery rhymes, songs, riddles, games, football yells, lyric poems, ballads, and mnemonic devices, as well as in poems of sophisticated reflection. In its several guises, it may be the most frequently used metrical form in English Poetry.

According to the hymnbooks, Common Measure consists of lines of 14 *syllables*, 7 of them stressed. As a type of *accentual* Folk Meter, however, it is more clearly a shortened variant of the Long Measure, the eighth stress being dropped:

$$- \ - \ - \ - \ \| \ - \ - \ -$$

But to understand what happens here we must take a look at another of the basic features of Folk Meters.

In poetry that has a large differential (poetry with a heavy beat), the stresses tend to fall at *apparently equal intervals of time*, regardless of the modality of the rhythm. In the passage

The girl in the *lóng dréss*
  —   —

Had a *lónger dréss*
 —   x   —

Than the girl with the *lónger addréss*
   —   x x   —

the stresses on "long" and "dress" tend to be separated by the
same time period whether two syllables intervene or none.

The more accurately a poem maintains such a chrono-
metric regularity of stresses, the more **isochronous** is its meter.
Isochronous means "composed of equal units of time," and
isochronism is more often than not one of the rhythmic and
metrical features of a poem in Folk Meter.

If a stress is missing, therefore, as it is in Common Measure,
we want to compensate for it in some way, *to fill up the time
period* it would have taken. One of the most striking features
of Folk Meter is this phenomenon of compensation. Suppose
you are asked to count aloud to seven. You would probably
count with a sense of some rhythm, such as:

> *one*   two   *three*   four   *five*   six   *seven*

Now suppose you are asked to count again, this time omitting
the fourth number. If you wanted to maintain the rhythm,
you would render:

> *one*   two   *three*   five   *six*   seven

The last three numbers do not receive the stresses they had in
the original pattern. What can you do, when dropping the
fourth word, to *compensate* for it, preserving the original
rhythmic relationship of the remaining stresses? You can

(1) *pause* for the appropriate length of time:

> *óne*   two   *thrée*   (*pause*)   *fivé*   six   *sevén*

(2) you can *hold* or draw out the pronunciation of the preceding number; you can even chant it or sing it, as long as you
consume the necessary time:

> *óne*   two   *thrée–yee*   *fivé*   six   *sevén*

(3) you can *indicate rhythmically* that you are starting a
new count:

> *óne*   two   *thrée*   **FÍVE**   six   *séven*

which is a kind of overriding syncopated technique. You give the impression that you will not wait until the fourth stress is fully compensated for, but still mean to maintain the proper stress-pattern.

While the cesura, then, is a *syntactic* or *logical* break, the **pause** (or hold, or compensating emphasis) at the end of the Folk Meter hemistich is a *metrical* or *musical* break, symbolized (p).

The proper diagram for Common Measure is therefore:

$$CM: \quad - \quad - \quad - \quad - \quad \| \quad - \quad - \quad - \quad (p)$$

or, printed in hemistichs:

$$- \quad - \quad - \quad - \quad \|$$
$$- \quad - \quad - \quad (p)$$

This pause cannot be found by an examination of the words on the page. It must be heard, by the ear or by the mind's ear.

	stresses	
	hemistich	*full-line*

The king sits in Dunfermlin town,

‿ ´   ‿   ´ ‖   4 ⎫
                              ⎬ 7
Sae merrily drinkin the wine:

‿ ´   ‿ (p)   3p ⎭

'Whare will I get a mariner,

‿   ´ ‿ ´ ‖   4 ⎫
                              ⎬ 7
Will sail this ship o mine?'

‿ ´ ‿ (p)   3p ⎭

Here the pause compensates for the missing secondary stress at the end of each line in the couplet. In terms of full-lines, the diagram is:

$$- \quad - \quad - \quad - \quad \| \quad - \quad - \quad - \quad (p)$$
$$- \quad - \quad - \quad - \quad \| \quad - \quad - \quad - \quad (p)$$

We often obey the pause "naturally" or unconsciously. If we did not, we would read the poem as though it were written:

The king sits in Dunfermlin town,
$$- \quad - \qquad - \qquad -$$

Sae merrily drinkin the wine: 'Whare
$$- \qquad - \qquad - \qquad \mathbf{-}$$

Will I get a mariner, will sail
$$- \qquad - \quad ? \qquad -$$

This ship o mine?' . . .?
$$- \qquad - \qquad ?$$

The meter would fall apart. In order to preserve the flow of stresses we are obliged to indicate (in one of the three ways) the start of a new count after the syllable "wine," which carries a primary stress but is followed immediately by another primary in "Whare." This is the only place in the stanza where two primaries are not separated by a secondary stress. *We use a pause (or equivalent) to compensate for the absence of that secondary stress.* We do so because we are aware that the rhythmic alternation nowhere else permits two primaries to come together. We do not want to jolt the thumping accents out of their beat any more than we would want suddenly to change pace when clapping hands rhythmically. The presence of the pause, then, depends partly on the alternation of primaries and secondaries.

Here are some examples of Common Measure:

With men who know tobacco best,
   −   −   −   −   ‖   4 ⎫

It's Whammos two to one.   7
     −   −   −   (p)   3p ⎭

Wéstron wínd, whén will thou blów?   4 ⎫
                                       7
The smáll rain dówn can ráin.   3p ⎭

Chríst, that my lóve were ín my árms,   4 ⎫
                                       7
And Í in my béd agáin.   3p ⎭

Súmer ís ycómen ín,   4

Lóude síng cuckóu!   3p

Gróweth séed and blóweth méed,   4

And spríngth the wóde nów.   3p

Our king has wróte a láng létter,   4

    And séaled it ówre with góld;   3p

He sént it tó my lórd Dunwáters,   4

    To réad it íf he cóuld.   3p

Hark, hark! the dogs do bark!
  The beggars are coming to town;
  Some in rags, and some in tags,
    And some in velvet gowns.

Her prétty féet	2
Like snáils did créep	2 } 4
A líttle óut, and thén,	3p
As if they playéd at bo-peep,	4
Did soon draw in again.	3p

(The print breaks the first hemistich into two quarter-lines. Pronouncing "playéd" with two syllables makes it easier to promote "at" to ictus.)

Sígh no more, ládies, sígh no móre,
  Mén were decéivers éver;
One foot in sea, and one on shore,
  To one thing constant never.
    Then sígh not só,
    But lét them gó,
  And be you blithe and bonny,
Converting all your sounds of woe
  Into Hey nonny, nonny.

(The full-lines are broken typographically according to the plan of the "internal" rhymes. In terms of the "end" rhyme, falling on every seventh stress, the poem is still in couplets, rhyming "ever-never" and "bonny-nonny.")

For Mercy has a human heart,
Pity a human face,
And Love, the human form divine,
And Peace, the human dress.

Gaily bedight,
    A gallant knight,
In súnshine ánd in shádow,
    Had journeyed long,
    Singing a song,
In séarch of Éldorádo.

I múst go dówn to the séas agáin,‖to the lónely séa and the ský,
And all I ask is a tall ship and a star to steer her by,
And the wheel's kick and the wind's song and the white sail's
    shaking,
And a grey mist on the sea's face and a grey dawn breaking.

(In full-lines. Notice the cesuras.)

    The yéllow fóg that rúbs its báck‖upón the wíndow-pánes,
    The yellow smoke that rubs its muzzle on the window-panes.

---

when mán detérmined tó destróy
himsélf he pícked the wás
of sháll and fínding ónly whý
smáshed it ínto becáuse

Straddling each a dolphin's back
And steadied by a fin,
Those Innocents re-live their death,
Their wounds open again.
The ecstatic waters laugh because
Their cries are sweet and strange,
Through their ancestral patterns dance,
And the brute dolphins plunge.

HALF MEASURE, HALF METER (HM)

The line which, for lack of an established term, we may call **Half Meter** (although the term "Short Meter," to be discussed later, is sometimes used), is relatively rare as a continuous form. But as a variation on one of the other folk lines, or as part of a complex stanza, it is quite popular.

The Half Measure line, when completely regular, has a total of 12 syllables, 6 stresses alternating with 6 slacks. *Each* hemistich contains 3 stresses plus a compensating pause. This means that the HM full-line contains a pause just before the cesura and another one at the end. The diagram for the full-line is then:

HM: − − − (p)‖ − − − (p)

or, printed in hemistichs:

− − − (p)‖

− − − (p)

The Half Meter has all the essential features of folk meter: it is divided at the center by a fixed cesura; it usually appears in couplets; the pauses compensate for missing stresses; stresses plus compensating pauses still preserve the basic eight-beat pattern; each hemistich normally contains two primary stresses.

This last feature is important and needs to be looked at more closely. With three stresses in the hemistich, the tendency is for the first and third to be primary and the middle one to be secondary:

1	2	3		4	5	6	*total stresses*
⸚	´	⸚	(p)‖	⸚	´	⸚ (p)	
1		2		3		4	*primary stresses*

thus preserving four primaries in the full-line, as all folk meters do.

The three-stress hemistich sometimes ends with a slack after the third stress. This slack is capable of being promoted, and can make a fourth stress. By the same token, the fourth stress of a *full* hemistich can sometimes be demoted to slack, forming a **short hemistich**. Some hemistichs, then, can be scanned either as Common Measure:

Taffy was a Wĕlshmán,
—   —   —   — ‖   4 ⎫

Taffy was a thief;   7
—   —   —   (p)   3 ⎭

Taffy came to mў hóuse
—   —   — — ‖   4 ⎫

And stole a piece of beef.   7
—   —   — (p)   3 ⎭

or as Half Measure:

Taffy was a Welshman,
—   —   —   (p)‖   3 ⎫

Taffy was a thief;   6
—   —   —   (p)   3 ⎭

Taffy came to my house
—   —   —   (p)‖   3 ⎫

And stole a piece of beef.   6
—   —   —   (p)   3 ⎭

It does not matter whether "man" and "house" are stressed or not. The important thing is to maintain the four *primary* stresses:

primary stresses

Taffy was a Welshman, Taffy was a thief;
—   —   ‖ —   —   4

Taffy came to my house and stole a piece of beef.
—   —   ‖   —   —   4

Here are some passages where Half Measure is at least a probable scansion:

Say me, wight in the broom,
　－　　　　－　　　　　　－　　(p)‖　　　　　3　⎫
　　　　　　　　　　　　　　　　　　　　　　　　　　⎬ 6
What is me for to doon?　　　　　　　　　　　　　⎭
　－　　　－　　　　－　(p)　　　　　　　　　3

Ich have the werste bonde
　－　　　　　　－　　－　　(p)‖　　　　　　3　⎫
　　　　　　　　　　　　　　　　　　　　　　　　　　⎬ 6
That is in any londe.　　　　　　　　　　　　　　⎭
　－　－　－　　　　(p)　　　　　　　　　　3

The fírst time they róde togéther,　　　　　3

Nów Sir Húgh and hé,　　　　　　　　　　3

He túrnd him ín his sáddle　　　　　　　　3

like an ápple ón a trée.　　　　　　　　　3

Ye Híghlands, ánd ye Láwlands,
　　Oh whére háve you béen?
They have slain the Earl of Murray,
　　And they layd him on the green.

'Now wáe be tó thee, Húntly!
　　And wherefore did you sae?
I bade you bring him wi you,
　　But forbáde you hím to sláy.'

She has twá wéel-made féet,
　　Far bétter ís her hánd;
She's as jímp ín the míddle
　　As óny wíllow-wánd.

The thief got off his horse,
  With courage stout and bold,
To séarch for the óld man's bág,
  And gáve him his hórse to hóld.

He opend this rogue's portmantle,
  It was glorious to behold;
There were three hundred pounds in silver,
  And three hundred pounds in gold.

There wás a gállant shíp,‖and a gállant shíp was shé   6

And shé wás cálled‖The Góulden Vánitíe.   6

(Printed in full-lines. You can read it as CM if you also stress "and" in line 1 and "The" in line 2.)

Strike up, you lusty gallants, with musick and sound of drum,
For we have descryed a rover, upon the sea is come;
His name is Captain Ward, right well it doth appear,
There hás not been súch a róver‖found óut this thóusand yéar.

(The difficulty in the fourth line is largely due to the unclearness of the cesura.)

Red-Cap he was there,
  And he was there indeed,
And he was standing by,
  With a red cap on his head.

Three wise men of Gotham
Went to sea in a bowl;
Íf the bówl had been strónger,
My sóng wóuld have been lónger.

There were cómfits ín the cábin,
    And apples in the hold;
The sails were made of silk,
    And the masts were made of gold.

I am monarch of all I survey,
    My right there is none to dispute;
From the centre all round to the sea,
    I am lord of the fowl and the brute.

No, nó, the útmost sháre
    Of mý desíre, shall bé
Onely to kisse that Aire,
    That lately kissèd thee.

(It is helpful to pronounce "kissèd" with two syllables.)

Break, break, break,
    On thy cóld gray stónes, O Séa!
And I wóuld that my tóngue could útter
    The thoughts that arise in me.

Sóme seed the bírds devóur,
    And some the season mars,
But here and there will flower
    The solitary stars.

Success is counted sweetest
By those who ne'er succeed.
To comprehend a nectar
Requires sorest need.

Thát woman's dáys were spént
In ígnoránt good-wíll,
Her níghts in árgumént
Untíl her vóice grew shríll.

Upón the bánk, she stóod   3
In the cóol   1 ⎫
Of spént emótions.   2 ⎭   ⎯⎯ 3
She félt, amóng the léaves,   3
The déw   1 ⎫ 3
Of óld devótions.   2 ⎭

(Note how the typography counterpoints the metrical structure.)

---

we are so both and oneful
night cannot be so sky
sky cannot be so sunful
i am through you so i

The glacier knocks in the cupboard,
    The desert sighs in the bed,
And the crack in the tea-cup opens
    A lane to the land of the dead.

O dárk dárk dárk.‖ They áll go ínto the dárk,   6
The vácant interstéllar spáces, the vácant ínto the vácant,
The cáptains, mérchant bánkers, éminent mén of létters,
The génerous pátrons of árt, the státesmen ánd the rúlers,
Distínguished cívil sérvants, cháirmen of mány commíttees,
Indústrial lórds and pétty cóntractors,‖áll go ínto the dárk,   7
And dárk the Sún and Móon, and the Álmanách de Gótha
And the Stóck Exchánge Gazétte, the Diréctory óf Diréctors.
(Not formally rhymed, but some HM characteristics remain.
Notice the four-stress hemistich variation in line 6.)

POULTER'S MEASURE (PM), SHORT MEASURE, SHORT METER (SM)

Short Meter (SM) is represented in the hymnals as consisting of four lines of 6–6–8–6 syllables respectively:

syllables

Bring justice to our land,	6
That all may dwell secure,	6
And finely build for days to come	8
Foundations that endure.	6

Poulter's Measure (PM), on the other hand, is sometimes defined as a couplet in which the first line contains 12 syllables and the second line 14 (the poulterer or egg-seller giving you a couple extra when you buy a second dozen). That is, Poulter's Measure has basically the same syllable-counts as Short Meter, only it is printed in full-lines.

But the number of *syllables* is not the most distinctive thing about either form. Both PM and SM normally have a fixed middle cesura, both rhyme the sixth stress with the thirteenth, both tend to alternate stresses and slacks, both lend themselves to the mingling of hemistichs of different lengths, both use compensatory pauses, and, most important of all, both have the same *stress*-pattern, the one printed in hemistichs and the other in full-lines. Thus, although the labels "Poulter's Measure" and "Short Meter" are often applied to syllable-counting types of meter (see the next chapter), they best apply to a fundamental metrical structure that is based on a carefully distributed stress-pattern. We can use the two terms interchangeably, to refer to a special combination of Folk Meter lines. Specifically, Poulter's Measure (or Short Meter) may best be defined as a couplet consisting of one line of Half Meter followed by one line of Common Measure:

stresses

$$PM \ (SM): \begin{cases} - \ - \ - \ (p)\| \ - \ - \ - \ (p) & 6 & HM \\ - \ - \ - \ -\| \ - \ - \ - \ (p) & 7 & CM \end{cases}$$

Or, printed in hemistichs:

− − − (p) ‖	3	} HM	
− − − (p).	3		} PM
	—	+	
− − − − ‖	4	} CM	
− − − (p).	3		

When Poulter's Measure appears in its strictest form, *twelvers* (twelve-syllable lines) alternating with *fourteeners*, the cesura sometimes becomes weak and may even drift away from its central position, and the pauses likewise tend to weaken or to disappear, especially from the twelvers. Usually, however, it will be recognizable by its distinctive stress-pattern of 6−7, more often printed as 3−3−4−3.

There is a tendency in PM for the thought of the third hemistich to run over into the fourth, the third being the only hemistich in the stanza without a required pause.

O Alva woods are bonnie,
　　−　　−　　　　−　　(p)‖　　　　　3
Tillycoultry hills are fair,
　　−　　−　　−　(p)　　　　3
But when I think on the braes o Menstrie
　　−　　−　　　　−　　　−　‖　4
It maks my heart aye sair.
　　−　　—　　−　(p)　　　　3

6 *HM*

7 *CM*

PM

The following examples give some idea of the great variety
of rhythmical effects available in Poulter's Measure:

I lothe that I did love,
–   –   –   (p)   ‖   3 ⎤
                                          ⎬ 6 *HM*
In youth that I thought swete,   ⎦   ⎤
–   .   –   –   (p)   3   ⎥
                                                    ⎥
As time requires: for my behove   ———   ⎬ *PM*
–   –   –   –   ‖   4 ⎤   ⎥
                                    ⎬ 7 *CM*   ⎦
Me thinkes they are not mete.   ⎦
–   –   –   (p)   3

Whán the brére was unbréd,   3 ⎤
                                          ⎬ 6
Thanne hádde ít no rínde;   3 ⎦

Whán the máiden hath thát she lóveth,   4 ⎤
                                          ⎬ 7
Shé is withóute longínge.   3 ⎦

(The second line may take a stress on the first syllable instead
of the second, and the third line may be read as three-stress.)

In he toke good Robyn,   3
And all his company: 3
'Welcome be thou, Robyn Hode,   4
Welcome arte thou to me.'   3

A: Then wórd is gáne to Léith,   3
      Álso to Édinburgh tówn,   3
      That the lády had kílld the láird,   3
      The láird o Wáristóun.   3

B: But wórd's gane dóun to Léith,   3
       And úp to Émbro tóun,   3
       That the lády shé has sláin the láird,   4
       The láird of Wáristóun.   3

(Version A is in Half Measure, Version B in Poulter's Measure.)

O sóme were pláying cárds,‖and sóme were pláying díce,   6

Whén he took óut an ínstrumént,‖bored thírty hóles at twíce.   7

(In full-lines.)

She cáres not fór her dáddy,
   Nor cáres she not fór her mámmy,
For she ís, she ís, she ís, she ís
   My lórd of Lówgave's lássy.

Cock a doodle doo!
My dame has lost her shoe;
My master's lost his fiddling-stick,
And knows not what to do.

Hót-cróss búns!‖hót-cróss búns!   6
Óne a pénny, twó a pénny,   4 ⎱
   Hót-cróss búns!   3 ⎰ 7
If you have no daughters,   3 ⎱
Give them to your sons,   3 ⎰ 6
One a penny, two a penny,   4 ⎱
   Hot-cross buns!   3 ⎰ 7

(This makes four full-lines in the 6–7–6–7 pattern, rhyming "buns-buns-sons-buns.")

An epicure, dining at Crewe,   3   } 6
Found quite a large mouse in his stew.   3

    Said the wáiter, "Don't shóut,   2 } 4 } 7
    And wáve it abóut,   2
Or the rest will be wanting one, too!"   3

(In terms of full-lines, this PM couplet rhymes "stew-too.")

Her Eyes the Glow-worme lend thee,
The Shooting Starres attend thee
    And the Élves alsó,
    Whose líttle eyes glów,
Like the sparks of fire, befriend thee.

The bustle in a house   3
The morning after death   3
Is sólemnést of índustríes   4
Enácted upón éarth,—   3

The sweeping up the heart,
And putting love away
We shall not want to use again
Until eternity.

(Notice the promotions in the last hemistich of each stanza.)

    Away in the loveable west,
    On a pastoral forehead of Wales,
I was únder a róof here, Í was at rést,
    And they the prey of the gales.

The garden flew round with the angel,
The angel flew round with the clouds,
And the clouds flew round and the clouds flew round
And the clouds flew round with the clouds.

LARGER STANZAS AND CONTINUOUS FORMS

It is the combining of different hemistichs that makes the Folk Meter so versatile. But how many kinds of hemistich are there, after all? Only two: one containing four stresses, and the other containing three plus a compensatory pause. The full-line can therefore be made in four possible combinations: 4–4, 4–3, 3–3, and (rarely) 3–4. The normal folk couplet, containing four hemistichs, appears most frequently in the patterns we have seen: 4–4–4–4 (Long Measure), 4–3–4–3 (Common Measure), 3–3–3–3 (Half Measure), and 3–3–4–3 (Poulter's Measure).

However, if the poet wants to add extra hemistichs to basic stanzas, he can achieve any number of combinations. He can also elaborate his stanzas by adding refrains or substituting two-stress **quarter-lines** for regular hemistichs:

1	"And whát wul ye léive to your báirns and your wífe,	4
2	Edward, Edward?	2
3	And what wul ye leive to your bairns and your wife,	4
4	Whan yé gang óvir the séa O?"	3
5	"The wárldis róom, late them bég thrae lífe,	4
6	Mither, mither,	2
7	The warldis room, late them beg thrae life,	4
8	For tháme nevir máir wul I sée O."	3

This symmetrically complex stanza is an elaboration and ornamentation of a simple folk couplet. Lines 2 and 6 are two-stress quarter-lines while lines 3 and 7 are repetitions. If we discount these lines we are left with a familiar basic pattern:

"And what wul ye leive to your bairns and your wife,	4
Whan ye gang ovir the sea O?"	3
"The warldis room, late them beg thrae life,	4
For thame nevir mair wul I see O."	3

with $\frac{3}{4}$ *CM* marked to the right.

As opposed to ornamental elaborations, the formal extension of the folk line beyond the couplet (or quatrain, if printed in broken lines) is usually done in one of two ways, continuously or stanzaically.

The **continuous** form merely repeats a staple line indefinitely, most commonly the seven-stress. Sometimes it is a mixture of seven- and six-stressers.

All délicate dáys and pléasant, all spírits and sórrows are cást   6
Far óut with the fóam of the présent that swéeps to the súrf of
the pást;   6
Where beyónd the extréme séa-wall, and betwéen the remóte
sea-gátes,   6
Wáste water wáshes, and táll ships fóunder, and déep death
wáits;   6
Where, míghty with déepening sídes, clad abóut with the séas as
with wíngs,   6
And impélled of invísible tídes, and fulfílled of unspéakable
thíngs,   6
White-éyed and póisonous-fínned, shark-tóothed and sérpentine-
cúrled,   6
Rolls, únder the whítening wínd of the fúture, the wáve of the
wórld.   6
The dépths stand náked in súnder behínd it, the stórms flee
awáy . . .   6

(Some metrists would not classify this passage as Folk Meter. Several of the cesuras are weak or nonmedial, and pauses are not always demanded after the third stress of the line.)

Through twénty hóles made tó his héarth at ónce blew twénty
páir   7
That fíred his cóals, sómetimes with sóft, sómetimes with
véhement áir,   7
Ás he wílled and his wórk requíred. Amíds the fláme he cást   7
Tin, sílver, précious góld, and bráss; and ín the stóck he pláced   7
A míghty ánvil; his ríght hánd a wéighty hámmer héld,   7
His léft his tóngs. And fírst he fórged a stróng and spácious
shíeld,   7

Adórned with twénty séveral húes; abóut whose vérge he béat   7
A ríng, thrée-fold and rádiánt, and ón the báck he sét   7

(The poet varies the cesura. The pauses have disappeared.)

When six-stress or seven-stress lines are in regular duple
rhythm, the syllable-counts are of course regular too, and the
lines are then describable as twelvers or fourteeners. Syllabic
labels are preferable where cesuras and pauses no longer hold
their fixed positions.

	stresses	*syllables*
O lét me bréathe a whíle, and hóld thy héavy hánd,	6	12
My grievous faults with shame enough I understand.	6	12
Take ruth and pity on my plaint, or else I am forlorn;	7	14
Let not the world continue thus in laughing me to scorn.	7	14
Madam, if I be he, to whom you once were bent,	6	12
With whom to spend your time sometime you were content:	6	12
If any hope be left, if any recompense	6	12
Be able to recover this forpassed negligence,	7	14
O, help me now poor wretch in this most heavy plight,	6	12
And furnish me yet once again with Tediousness to fight.	7	14

As we have seen, when the couplet has a consistent stress-
count of 6−7 it makes accentual Poulter's Measure:

The núrse depárted ónce, the chámber dóor shut clóse   6 ⎫ PM
Assúréd thát no líving wíght her dóing míght disclóse,   7 ⎭
She pourèd fórth intó the víal óf the fríar   6̄
Wáter, óut of a sílver éwer that ón the bóard stood bý her. 7
The sleepy mixture made, fair Juliet doth it hide   6̄
Únder her bólster sóft, and só untó her béd she híed: 7

Where divers novel thoughts arise within her head,   6
And shé is só envíronéd abóut with déadly dréad   7

Each beast can choose his fere according to his mind,
And eke can show a friendly chere, like to their beastly kind.
A lion saw I late, as white as any snow,
Which seemèd well to lead the race, his port the same did show.
Upon the gentle beast to gaze it pleasèd me,
For still methought he seemèd well of noble blood to be.
And as he pranced before, still seeking for a make,
As who would say 'There is none here, I trow, will me forsake',
I might perceive a wolf as white as whalésbone,
A fairer beast, a fresher hue, beheld I never none,
Save that her looks were fierce and froward eke her grace:
Toward the which this gentle beast gan him advance apace,
And with a beck full low he bowèd at her feet
In humble wise, as who would say 'I am too far unmeet'.

Of the **stanzaic** methods of extending the folk meters, one
of the simplest is that of doubling the couplet to make a
quatrain of full-lines. Such **doubled** stanzas can be abbreviated LMD, CMD, HMD, and PMD.

CMD:

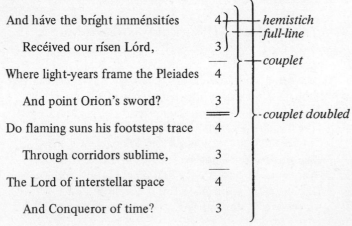

And háve the bríght imménsitíes	4	hemistich / full-line
Recéived our rísen Lórd,	3	couplet
Where light-years frame the Pleiades	4	
And point Orion's sword?	3	
Do flaming suns his footsteps trace	4	couplet doubled
Through corridors sublime,	3	
The Lord of interstellar space	4	
And Conqueror of time?	3	

Other ways of stanzaically augmenting Folk Meter are difficult to generalize about because they take so many forms, combining different folk lines, hemistichs, and quarter-lines.

Within the basic Folk Meter structure, a very large range of tone and movement is possible. Compare, for example, the rhythmic and tonal effects of two stanzas in the same variant of meter (1 LM plus 1 CM):

A: 'Twas brillig, and the slithy toves   4 ⎫ 8 *LM*
        Did gyre and gimble in the wabe: 4 ⎭
     All mimsy were the borogoves,   4 ⎫ 7 *CM*
        And the mome raths outgrabe.   3 ⎭

B: But now go the bells, and we are ready,   4 ⎫ 8
     In one house we are sternly stopped   4
     To say we are vexed at her brown study,   4 ⎫ 7
     Lying so primly propped.   3

Here are samplings of modified folk lines:

I set her on my pacing steed,   4
    And nothing else saw all day long;   4
For sideways would she lean, and sing   4
    A faery's song.   2

(The quarter-line leaves the folk couplet incomplete.)

_____

I've known her from an ample nation   4
Chŏose óne;   2 (1)
Then close the valves of her attention   4
Líke stóne.   2 (1)

(A couplet where both lines are incomplete.)

_____

If you can't answer my questions nine—	4
Sing ninety-nine and ninety!	3
Oh you're not God's you're one of mine.	4
And the crów flies óver the whíte oak trée!	4

Oh what is higher than the tree?	4
Sing ninety-nine and ninety!	3
And what is deeper than the sea?	4
And the crow flies over the white oak tree!	4

(In mixtures of 3-stress and 4-stress hemistichs, it is uncommon for the stanza to conclude with a 4-stresser. Notice that the second and fourth lines of each stanza are parentheses or refrains; if they are taken as superstructure, the base structure would be one full-line of LM.)

_____

But, Móusie, thóu art nó thy láne,	4
In proving foresight may be vain:	4
The best-laid schemes o' mice an' men,	4
Gang aft agley,	2
An' lea'e us nought but grief an' pain	4
For promis'd joy!	2

(This stanzaic form, with the rhyme-scheme *aaabab*, is called the *Burns Meter* or *Burns Stanza*.)

_____

His sheeld was al of gold so reed,	4
And thérinne wás a bóres héed,	4
A charbocle by his syde;	3
And there he swoor on ale and breed	4
How that the geaunt shal be deed,	4
Bityde what bityde!	3

(This stanza, called the *Romance Six*, shares the effects of LM: 4–4–3–4–4–3– and of CM: 4–4–3–4–4–3.)

_____

With throats unslaked, with black lips baked,	4
We could nor laugh nor wail;	3
Through utter drought all dumb we stood!	4
I bit my arm, I sucked the blood,	4
And cried, A sail! a sail!	3

The effect here is not merely of adding to the basic CM stanza, but of *suspending its resolution* for one hemistich. When the expectation of concluding on a three-stress hemistich is set up strongly, the *suspense* can be held for a number of lines:

She fears him, and will always ask	4
What fated her to choose him;	3
She meets in his engaging mask	4
All reasons to refuse him;	3
But what she meets and what she fears	4
Are less than are the downward years,	4 ⎤ *suspended*
Drawn slowly to the foamless weirs	4 ⎦ *resolution*
Of age, were she to lose him.	3

Three blind mice!	3
See how they run!	3
They all ran after the farmer's wife,	4
Who cut off their tails with a carving knife.	4
Did you ever see such a sight in your life	4
As three blind mice?	3

The augmented folk meter is often sensitive to even slight changes. Here is a stanza composed almost completely of three's, where the presence of a single four gives rhythmic individuality to the entire pattern:

When I am dead, my dearest,	3
Sing no sad songs for me;	3
Plant thou no roses at my head,	4

Nor shady cypress tree.   3
Be the green grass above me   3
  With showers and dewdrops wet;   3
And if thou wilt, remember,   3
  And if thou wilt, forget.   3

(The easiest scansion is one PM plus one HM couplet, a pattern reinforced by the punctuation.)

The possibilities for further elaboration of the folk couplet are evident:

Fear no more the heat o' the sun,   4
  Nor the furious winter's rages;   3
Thou thy worldly task hast done,   4
  Home art gone, and ta'en thy wages: 4
Golden lads and girls all must,   4
As chimney-sweepers, come to dust.   4

Under the greenwood tree   3
Who loves to lie with me,   3
And turn his merry note   3
Unto the sweet bird's throat,   3
Come hither, come hither, come hither: 3 /
    Here shall he see   2
    No énemý   2
But wínter and róugh wéather.   3

Full fathom five thy father lies;   4
  Of his bónes are córal máde;   3
Those are pearls that were his eyes: 4
  Nóthing of hím that doth fáde,   3
Bút doth súffer a séa chánge   3 (4)
Ínto sómething rích and stránge.   3 (4)

Sea nymphs hourly ring his knell:	4
Ding-dong.	2
Hárk! now I héar them—Díng-dong, béll.	4

(A number of ambiguous lines that can be read either as 4-stress or 3-stress.)

Have you séen but a bríght lily grów	3
Befóre rude hánds have tóuched it?	3
Ha' you marked but the fall o' the snow	3
Before the soil hath smutched it?	3
Ha' you felt the wool of beaver,	3
Or swán's down éver?	2
Or have smelt o' the bud o' the briar?	3
Or the nárd in the fire?	2
Or have tasted the bag of the bee?	3
O so whíte! O so sóft! O so swéet is shé!	4

A route of evanescence	3
With a revolving wheel;	3
A résonánce of émeråld,	3 (4)
A rush of cochineal;	3
And every blossom on the bush	4
Adjusts its tumbled head,—	3
The mail from Tunis, probably,	4
An easy morning's ride.	3

We should remember again to make the distinction between rhythm and meter. Going by rhythmical "flavor" alone, we may feel that some of the examples in this chapter have nothing in common with others, until we realize what a great variety of rhythms can be created within the basic metrical framework of the Folk Meter. Within each of the four main forms, some poems keep a strict count of the syllables—hence such terms as *twelver*, *fourteener*, and *sixteener*—and maintain a steady duple rhythm. Others fall into triple rhythms or move from duple to triple, either arbitrarily or at set places, as at the beginning or end of the line or hemistich. Many also fall into **single rhythm**, where the stresses are not separated by any slacks at all. Look at the rhythmic freedom in the line

The king sits in Dunfermlin town, Sae merrily drinkin the wine
x — — x x — x —   x — xx — x x —
 1 2   3   4   5   6   7

where we are given *single rhythm* between stresses 1 and 2; *duple rhythm* (also called *common rhythm*) between stresses 3 and 4, 4 and 5; and *triple rhythm* between stresses 2 and 3, 5 and 6, 6 and 7. We normally refer to this "logaoedic" mixture of rhythms as **tumbling** or **duple-triple** rhythm, even where single rhythms are also involved. And all this rhythmic variation occurs within a single basic meter.

THE DIPODIC PRINCIPLE

There is, in most folk-meter poems, an interesting rhythmical characteristic which occurs so regularly that it may be considered a standard metrical law of the folk lines. It has to do with the tendency of the primary stresses to alternate with secondary stresses, and the tendency of the full-line always to contain four primaries regardless of the number of secondaries. These features can be explained in terms of the **Dipodic Principle**, a somewhat involved dimension of the Folk Meters that we must look at now.

The concept of dipodics is best approached through the isochronous principle, which holds that, in poems where it applies, the metrical stresses are kept apart by equal intervals of time in our pronunciation. Let us take a line of three strong stresses:

Péas pórridge in the pót

We will tend to keep the stresses isochronously spaced, although the first and second ones are not separated by any slacks while the second and third are separated by three. If we insist on following the strong three-stress pattern begun by the metrical context, we will read:

Péas pórridge hót,	3
Péas pórridge cóld,	3
Péas pórridge in the pót,	3
Níne dáys óld.	3

But we will probably want to read the line with four stresses, making an accentual Poulter's Measure:

Péas pórridge hót,	3
Péas pórridge cóld,	3
Péas pórridge *ín* the pót	4
Níne dáys óld.	3

We can easily do so by promoting "in." In preserving the isochrony, we double the elapsed time between "por" and "pot" and increase the number of time units from two to three without adding a single syllable to the line.

Again, suppose we want to give three stresses to:

Fóur and twénty bláckbirds

The final syllable is quietly included after the third stress. But if we want to read the line with four stresses:

Fóur and twénty bláck bírds

we stretch out the pronunciation of "black" or pause after it, to keep up the isochronous beat.

With choices like this, how are we to resolve ambiguities?

1	Sing a song of sixpence,	?
2	A pocket full of rye;	3
3	Four-and-twenty blackbirds	?
4	Baked in a pie!	3

5 When the pie was opened	?
6 The birds began to sing;	3
7 Wasn't that a dainty dish	?
8 To set before the king?	3

If the odd-numbered lines are meant to be three-stress, calling for the scansion "síxpence," "bláckbirds," and "ópened," we are in trouble because we cannot deal comfortably with "dainty dish," which seems to require two stresses. On the other hand, if the odd-numbered lines are meant to be four-stress, calling for "dáinty-dísh," "síxpénce," and "bláckbírds," we are confronted with "opened," which would require a good amount of stretching to carry two stresses. Ought we to give these lines three stresses or four?

We may give either, because it does not matter. The true structure does not depend on whether the hemistich has three or four stresses, but rather on whether it has exactly two *primary* stresses:

primary stresses

Síng a song of síxpence,	2
A pócket full of rýe;	2
Fóur-and-twenty bláckbirds	2
Báked in a píe!	2

The basic measure or "foot" of the regularly isochronous folk line consists of one primary stress plus one secondary stress or its equivalent (in a pause or hold). This two-stress foot is a **dipod**. A poem where primaries and secondaries alternate regularly is called **dipodic verse**. The skeletal structure of the dipodic foot can be diagramed as | ˝ ´ | or as | ´ ˝ |. The two stresses may be separated by one, two, or no slacks, or possibly three.

The primary stress must be present. The secondary stress may be missing, in which case it is replaced by a pause:

| ˝ (p) |

Dipodically, the feet | ⌣́ ⌣̀ | and | ⌣́ (p) | are equivalent, so it does not matter whether we scan

blackbirds   or   blackbirds.
| ⌣́ ⌣̀ | | ⌣́   (p) |

The primary stress in a dipodic foot is the **thesis**, and the secondary stress is the **arsis**. When the arsis is followed by the thesis, it creates a **rising dipod**; when the thesis is followed by the arsis it creates a **falling dipod**:

falling dipod: | ⌣́ ⌣̀ | or | ⌣́ (p) |

rising dipod: | ⌣̀ ⌣́ |

We have seen how frequently, in the Folk Meters, the primaries and secondaries fall into regular alternation. It remains for us now to place them, as *theses* and *arses*, into the proper *dipodic* divisions:

Long Meter:

	total di-	
	stresses	*pods*

Our king he has a secret to tell, And ay well keepit it
⌣́   ⌣̀| ⌣́   ⌣̀ ‖ ⌣̀   ⌣̀ ‖⌣̀

must be:
⌣́   8   4

The English lords are coming down To dance and
⌣́   ⌣̀ | ⌣́   ⌣̀ ‖   ⌣́

win the victory.
⌣̀| ⌣́ ⌣̀   8   4

Common Meter:

	total stresses	*dipods*

The king sits in Dunfermlin town, Sae merrily
˘ ´ | ˘   ´ ‖   ˘

drinkin the wine:
´ | ˘ (p)   7   4

'Whare will I get a mariner, Will sail this ship o
˘   ´| ˘ ´ ‖   ˘   ´ |

mine?'
˘ (p)   7   4

Half Meter:

There were comfits in the cabin,   And apples
˘   ´ | ˘ (p) ‖   ˘

in the hold;
´ | ˘ (p)   6   4

The sails were made of silk,   And the masts
˘   ´ | ˘ (p) ‖   ˘

were made of gold.
´ | ˘ (p)   6   4

Poulter's Measure:

The bustle in a house   The morning after death
˘   ´| ˘ (p) ‖   ˘   ´ | ˘ (p)   6   4

Is solemnest of industries   Enacted upon earth.
˘   ´ | ˘   ´ ‖   ˘   ´| ˘ (p)   7   4

Whether the total stresses in the full-line number six, seven, or eight, there are always four dipods, ruled by the four primary stresses that the true folk line requires. This means

that in Half Meter four of the six stresses must be primary.
Two of them are thus compelled to be adjacent:

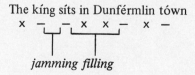

But *the isochronous time-distance between primaries must be
maintained by a pause or some other compensation.* In this
line we must maintain the primary-stress isochrony by *pausing*
where the secondary stress is lacking:

$$\overset{..}{} \quad \overset{.}{} \quad \underline{\overset{..}{} \,(p) \,\overset{..}{}} \quad \overset{.}{} \quad \overset{..}{}\,(p)$$

which gives us a line of four dipods:

$$\overset{..}{} \quad \overset{.}{} \mid \overset{..}{}\,(p)\| \quad \overset{..}{} \quad \overset{.}{} \mid \overset{..}{}\,(p)$$

The principle of isochronism is important in other ways. If
there are few or no slacks between stresses we need to pause
or hold to counteract the **jamming** of stresses together. If, on
the other hand, there are many slacks between stresses, we
need to hurry through all of them to counteract the **filling** of
slacks between stresses. Even relatively smooth duple-triple
rhythms have a certain amount of filling and jamming:

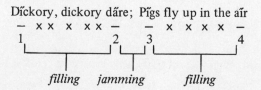

But these features are clearest on the dipodic level:

Primaries 1 and 2 are separated by five syllables, and 3 and 4 by four syllables, but the elapsed time is equivalent to that between 2 and 3, which are adjacent.

Syncopation is, theoretically, the *displacement* of a stress from a fixed isochronous position. Actually, however, it is the *tendency* of a stress to pull away from its isochronous position; whether we pronounce the stress with displacement or with compensation (e.g., hurrying or pausing) as we recite the poem is a choice in performance, not structural description.

Suppose we had:

Díckory, díckory dắre;‖The píg flew úp in the aír;

The mán in brówn soon bróught him dówn;‖hế wás thếre.

The fourth hemistich (the last three words) may be considered syncopated. The stresses are adjacent, while the established pace and the rhythmical nature of the language had led us to expect a number of slacks between them. The second primary ("there") comes too soon.

Syncopation is even more noticeable when the secondary stress between primaries is a promotion of an otherwise unimportant syllable.

1 Beat an empty barrel with the handle of a broom,
   ⏝   ⏝́ | ⏝   ⏝́ ‖   ⏝   ⏝́| ⏝ (p) 7

2 Hard as they were able,
   ⏝   ⏝́| ⏝ (p)   3

3 Boom, boom, BOOM.
   ⏝   ⏝́ | ⏝ →   (4)

4 With a silk umbrella and the handle of a broom,
  ← ⏝́ | ⏝   ⏝́| ⏝   ⏝́ ‖   ⏝   ⏝́| ⏝ (p) (7)

5 Boomlay, boomlay, boomlay, BOOM.
   ⏝   ⏝́| ⏝   ⏝́ ‖ ⏝ ⏝́ | ⏝(p)   7 (or 4)

6 THEN I had religion,   THEN I had a vision.
   ⏝   ⏝́| ⏝ (p)‖ ⏝   ⏝́| ⏝ (p)   6

7 I could not turn from their revel in derision.
   ˵ ˊ| ˵ ˊ ‖   ˵ ˊ| ˵ (p)   7

8 THEN I SAW THE CONGO,   CREEPING
   ˵   ˊ| ˵ (p)‖ ˵

   THROUGH THE BLACK,
   ˊ | ˵ (p)   6

9 CUTTING THROUGH THE FOREST WITH A
   ˵   ˊ | ˵   ˊ ‖

   GOLDEN TRACK.
   ˵ ˊ| ˵ (p)   7

10 Then along that riverbank
   ˵ ˊ | ˵ ˊ   4

11 A thousand miles
   ˵ ˊ | ˵ (p)   3

12 Tattooed cannibals danced in files
   ˵ ˊ |˵ ˊ ‖ ˵ ˊ|ˊ (p)   7

The passage in several places has a | ˵ ˊ ˵ | pattern unrelieved
by any slack syllables. In two of these the syncopating effect
is minor, "cŏuld nót tŭrn" (line 7) and "dańced ĭn fĭles" (line
12), as the middle secondary stress falls on a meaningful syllable and allows a logically rendered phrase. A strong syncopation appears, however, in "gŏldén tră̆ck" (line 9), "thŏusańd
mĭles" (line 11), and "tă̆ttoóed că̆n" (line 12), where the
secondary stress had been promoted from slack in the first
place merely to satisfy the meter, to keep the distance
between dipodic stresses.

This kind of syncopation is almost always achieved through
the device of jamming. The opposite technique, syncopation
through filling, so that the stress tends to come isochronously
late, is not common: if the line contains additional syllables
we often simply assign more stresses to it.

In some poems the **ground rhythm**, made of all the stresses,
is the one we naturally listen to; in others it is the dipodic or
primary rhythm. Sometimes the pattern of ground stresses is
confusing or obscure. We may not know whether the last
syllable of a hemistich ought to be a secondary or a slack or

whether the cesura needs to come after the third or the fourth
stress. But the dipodic or primary pattern, undisturbed by
these difficulties, may emerge in a familiar form.

ground stresses   *primary stresses*

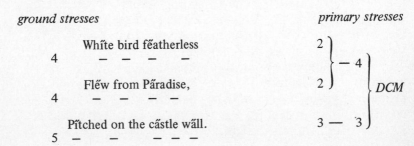

The ground pattern here consists of a mixture of stresses,
including the uncommon five-stress, while the pattern of
primary stresses is the clear 4–3 of Common Measure. Since
this is primary or dipodic rhythm, we will abbreviate it DCM.
(Thus, for example, DCMD would mean "Dipodic Common
Measure Doubled.") Note the new **primary pause.**

   Here are more cases where the meter of the poem takes
shape only on the primary level of stress:

ground stresses   *primary stresses*

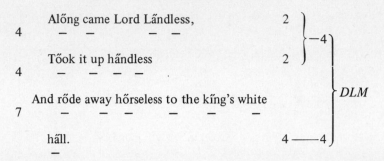

4   Alŏng came Lord Lăndless,   2 ⎫
     − −   − −   ⎬ −4 ⎫
                                                     ⎪   ⎪
4   Tŏok it up hăndless   2 ⎭   ⎪
     − − − − .   ⎪
                                                         ⎬ DLM
7   And rŏde away hŏrseless to the kĭng's white   ⎪
     − − − − − − −   ⎪
                                                         ⎪
     hăll.   4 ——4 ⎭
     −

---

ground stresses   *primary/dipodic stresses*

6   If you're ŏff to Philadĕlphia in the mŏrning,   3 ⎫
     − −   − − − −   ⎪
                                                         ⎪
5   You mŭstn't take my stŏries for a gŭide.   3 ⎪
     − − − − −   ⎬ ——DPM
                                                         ⎪
7   There's lĭttle left, indĕed, of the cĭty you will rĕad   4
     − − − − − − −   ⎪
                                                         ⎪
     of,   ⎪
                                                         ⎪
5   And ăll the folk I wrĭte about have dĭed.   3 ⎭
     − − − − −

7   Now fĕw will understănd if you mĕntion Talleyrănd, 4 ⎫
     − − − − − −   ⎪
                                                          ⎪
6   Or remĕmber what his cŭnning and his skĭll did;   3 ⎪
     − − − − − −   ⎬ ——DCM
                                                          ⎪
8   And the căbmen at the whărf do not knŏw Count   ⎪
     − − − − − −   ⎪
                                                          ⎪
     Zinzendŏrf,   4 ⎪
     − −   ⎪
                                                          ⎪
6   Nor the Chŭrch in Philadĕlphia he bŭilded.   3 ⎭
     − − − − −

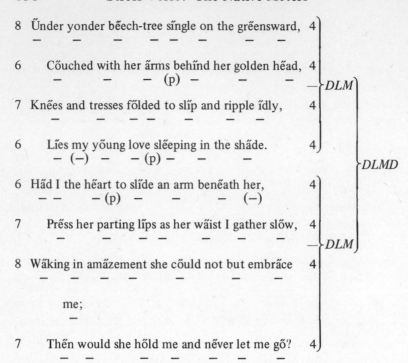

8   Únder yonder běech-tree síngle on the grěensward,   4

6   Cőuched with her ãrms behínd her golden hĕad,   4

7   Kněes and tresses főlded to slíp and ripple ïdly,   4

6   Lïes my yőung love slěeping in the shãde.   4

6   Hãd I the hĕart to slíde an arm beněath her,   4

7   Prěss her parting líps as her wãist I gather slőw,   4

8   Wãking in amãzement she cőuld not but embrãce   4

     me;

7   Thĕn would she hőld me and nĕver let me gő?   4

(The scansion of the ground stresses here is approximate, since it has much to do with the manner of recitation. That is, the ground rhythm is very ambiguous and the performer must make his own decisions: it is even possible to read the entire passage as Half Meter, with full pauses at the middle and end of the lines. On the dipodic or primary level, the four-stress pattern is clear and stable. The structure of the Dipodic Long Measure is reinforced by the rhymes *xaxa xbxb*, which if printed in *dipodic* full-lines would become the standard couplets *aa bb*.)

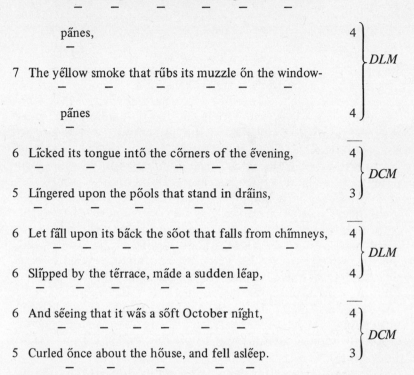

7   The yĕllow fog that rŭbs its back upŏn the window-

pānes,   4 ⎤
                                                             ⎥ DLM
7   The yĕllow smoke that rŭbs its muzzle ŏn the window-   ⎥

pānes   4 ⎦

6   Lĭcked its tongue intŏ the cŏrners of the ĕvening,   4 ⎤
                                                             ⎥ DCM
5   Lĭngered upon the pŏols that stand in drāins,   3 ⎦

6   Let fāll upon its băck the sŏot that falls from chĭmneys, 4 ⎤
                                                                 ⎥ DLM
6   Slĭpped by the tĕrrace, māde a sudden lĕap,   4 ⎦

6   And sĕeing that it wăs a sŏft October nĭght,   4 ⎤
                                                             ⎥ DCM
5   Curled ŏnce about the hŏuse, and fell aslĕep.   3 ⎦

The difference between ground level and dipodic level, then, provides one more dimension in which the poet can achieve contrapuntal relationships between a fixed, overriding pattern and a more varied, sensitive rhythm.

CHAPTER V

SYLLABIC VERSE

Syllabic verse is that in which the "meter" simply measures the total number of syllables in the line without any regard to stresses or slacks. Syllabic verse as a technical term may best be reserved for cases where the syllable-count is the *main* organizing element, since whenever a fixed number of stresses or feet occurs in a constant rhythm, there will be syllabic regularity. Just as stress-verse is seen most clearly where the total number of syllables per line is most variable, so syllabic verse is clearest where the number of stresses varies. Indeed, it is the capacity of syllabic verse for containing within a fixed line length a great variety of stresses, rhythms, kinds of diction, modal shifts, tempos, and so on, that has helped it to persevere as a form. It allows the poet freedom in rhythmic effects and yet keeps the syllabic organization under control, although its immediate effect upon the reader is more visual than auditory.

It may be argued that we cannot really appreciate syllable-counting as a form of organization because we cannot "hear" the duration of a full line of syllables; we listen rather for the pulsation of stresses. But when the stress-pattern becomes confused or unpredictable, we may appreciate the control of a fixed syllable-count. The common terms referring to the number of syllables in a word or a line are:

1 syllable	**monosyllabic**
more than 1	**polysyllabic**
2 syllables	**disyllabic**
3 "	**trisyllabic**
7 "	**heptasyllabic**
8 "	**octosyllabic**

9 syllables	nonosyllabic
10 "	decasyllabic
11 "	hendecasyllabic
12 "	duodecasyllabic or twelver
13 "	thirteener
14 "	fourteener
15 "	fifteener
16 "	sixteener

As in the extension of folk lines, *continuous* and *stanzaic* forms are used to extend the syllabic line into syllabically regular or predictable verse. The continuous forms measure out one line after the other according to some syllabic standard; they may be grouped into verse paragraphs. The stanzaic form can use the same device, but, as we shall see, it may also involve the **mating** of lines from stanza to stanza by virtue of identical syllable-counts.

CONTINUOUS FORMS

Here is a brief sampling of the most common types of syllabic line:

Octosyllabics (Eight Syllables)

The eight-syllable line, usually carrying four stresses, has been standard:

> Let us roll all our strength, and all
> Our sweetness, up into one ball;
> And tear our pleasures with rough strife
> Thorough the iron gates of life.
> Thus, though we cannot make our sun
> Stand still, yet we will make him run.

(Notice that "thorough" is disyllabic.) A common variation in English octosyllabics is the 4s heptasyllabic.

Seven-syllable Lines

The old question of whether the pattern | − x − x − x − | is
iambic tetrameter truncated or trochaic tetrameter catalectic
can be avoided by thinking of the line as duple-rhythm
heptasyllabic. This form has also been popular and, when
scanned as a truncated iambic, has been called an **upcast**
line:

> − |x − | x − |x   −   *7 syllables*
> While I draw this fleeting breath−   *(4 stresses)*
>
> When my eye-strings break in death−
>
> When I soar to worlds unknown−
>
> See Thee on thy judgment-throne−
>
> **Rock** of ages, cleft for me,
>
> Let me hide myself in Thee!

If we reverse the pattern to | x − x − x − x | we reduce the
tetrameter to trimeter and surround the stresses with slacks.
But we retain the constancy of the syllable-count:

> x − | x − |x   − | x   *7 syllables*
> Confirm my deeds and guide me: *(3 stresses)*
>
> My day, with thee beside me,
>
> Beginning, middle, ending,
>
> Will all be upward tending.

In this passage the heptasyllabic norm is more obvious
because the rhythmic pattern is unclear:

> It has happened suddenly,
> by surprise, in an arbor,
> or while drinking good coffee,
> after speaking, or before,

that I dumbly inhabit
a density; in language
nothing is to prevent it,
nothing to retain an edge.

Decasyllabics (Ten Syllables)

Most ten-syllable lines can be scanned as foot-verse, but
where such scansion becomes very rough it is sometimes
sufficient to note the syllabic norm:

> I wake and feel the fell of dark, not day.
> What hours, O what black hoürs we have spent
> This night! what sights you, heart, saw; ways you went!
> And more must, in yet longer light's delay.
>   With witness I speak this. But where I say
> Hours I mean years, mean life. And my lament
> Is cries countless, cries like dead letters sent
> To dearest him that lives alas! away.

(Notice how the poet extends "hours" to two syllables in the
second line.)

Hendecasyllabics (Eleven Syllables)

This is any line of eleven syllables. But the term has also
been used for such particular forms as

  a) iambic pentameter with feminine ending;

  b) iambic pentameter with an extra slack anywhere in the
  line;

  c) iambic pentameter with a fixed pattern of substitutions
  and an extra slack at a fixed place in the line;

  d) an eleven-syllable line with a fixed metrical scheme.

For example:

> One drop fell from a fern, and lo, a ripple
> Shook whatever it was lay there at bottom,

Blurred it, blotted it out. What was that whiteness?
Truth? A pebble of quartz? For once, then, something.

As a form of (c), this passage is rendered iambic pentameter with two trochaic inversions and a feminine ending:

— x | — x | x — | x — | x — | x

Yet the simplest metrical description is (d): trochaic pentameter with dactylic substitution in the second foot:

— x | — x x | — x | — x | — x

CONTINUOUSLY ALTERNATING FORMS

Another kind of continuous syllabic form is created by the *alternation* of syllabic lengths. For example, *syllabic* Poulter's Measure, which often has the same 6 + 7 stress-pattern and fixed cesura as *accentual* Poulter's Measure, is only distinguishable from it by the fixed regularity of its 12 + 14 syllable-count:

Syllabic Poulter's Measure:

When Súmmer tóok in hánd‖the wínter tó assáil   *12er*
With fórce of míght and vírtue gréat,‖his stórmy blásts to
    qúail,   *14er*
And when he clothèd fair the earth about with green,   *12er*
And every tree new garmented, that pleasure was to seen,   *14er*
Mine heart gan new revive, and changèd blood did stir   *12er*
Me to withdraw my winter woes, that kept within my dore. *14er*

With alternating syllable-counts as his only restriction, the poet can achieve considerable freedom of rhythm and phrasing:

4-syllable lines alternating with 2-syllable lines:

except in your
honour,
my loveliest,
nothing
may move may rest
—you bring

(out of dark the
earth)a
procession of
wonders
huger than prove
our fears

MATED FORMS (STANZAIC)

Mated syllabic forms must depend on stanzaic structure, since each line in the stanza must have the same syllable-count as the corresponding line (its *mate*) in the other stanzas. The sense of organization comes through a growing awareness of a *sequence* of syllable-counts. The devices of using enjambment in syllabic verse and of varying the stress-pattern while the syllable-count remains stable give some poems a distinctive appearance among metered forms:

	syllables
Although the aepyornis	7
or roc that lived in Madagascar, and	10
the moa are extinct,	6
the camel-sparrow, linked	6
with them in size—the large sparrow	8
Xenophon saw walking by a stream—was and is	12
a symbol of justice.	6

This bird watches his chicks with	7
a maternal concentration—and he's	10
been mothering the eggs	6
at night six weeks—his legs	6
their only weapon of defence.	8
He is swifter than a horse; he has a foot hard	12
as a hoof; the leopard	6

is not more suspicious. How	7
could he, prized for plumes and eggs and young, used	10
even as a riding-	6
beast, respect men hiding	6
actor-like in ostrich-skins, with	8
the right hand making the neck move as if alive and	13
from a bag the left hand	6

strewing grain, that ostriches	7
might be decoyed and killed! Yes this is he	10
whose plume was anciently	6
the plume of justice; he	6
whose comic duckling head on its	8
great neck revolves with compass-needle nervousness	12
when he stands guard, in S-	6

like foragings as he is	7
preening the down on his leaden-skinned back.	10
The egg piously shown	6
as Leda's very own	6
from which Castor and Pollux hatched,	8
was an ostrich-egg. And what could have been more fit	12
for the Chinese lawn it	6

(Note that the syllabic form allows some variation just as other forms do.)

The mating of lines syllabically is also used to construct **shaped poetry**:

Easter Wings

syllables

Lord, who createdst man in wealth and store,	10
Though foolishly he lost the same,	8
Decaying more and more	6
Till he became	4
Most poor;	2
With thee	2
Oh, let me rise	4
As larks, harmoniously,	6
And sing this day thy victories;	8
Then shall the fall further the flight in me.	10
My tender age in sorrow did begin;	10
And still with sicknesses and shame	8
Thou didst so punish sin,	6
That I became	4
Most thin.	2
With thee	2
Let me combine,	4
And feel this day thy victory;	8
For if I imp my wing on thine,	8
Affliction shall advance the flight in me.	10

(Note the variation in the third line from the last.)

CHAPTER VI
FREE VERSE

The term **free verse** implies a freedom from some restriction. But this alone does not differentiate it from any other form: stress-verse can be free from syllabic regularity, syllabic verse from stress-count, foot-verse from alliteration, alliterative verse from end-rhyme, and so on. Free verse, as a matter of fact, is an extremely general term that has been used to mean many different things, and trying to determine what all free verse poems have in common can be difficult.

One approach to the problem is to distinguish between two kinds of organization or form in poetry. *Organic form* uses patterns that seem to support, or be required by, the poem's meaning. *Abstract form* is made of patterns that are determined not by meaning but by an arbitrary choice of design or of mathematical relationship. Organic form is considered *part* of the meaning, so that a line with surprising content might use some surprising metrical effects. Abstract form is considered a *texture* of the meaning, so that the poet's fluctuating emotions may be put into perspective by, or given substance by contrast to, the constancy of an unaffected meter. The two of course overlap in good poetry, but traditional meters function mainly as abstract forms: the presence of an iambic pentameter in the middle of a poem is accounted for not by the meaning of that line, but by the fact that all the other lines in the poem are also iambic pentameter; it is simply maintaining a mathematical relationship.

Abstract form is restrictive or *counterlogical*: it remains relatively stable, while the "logical meaning" of the poem is relatively free. In the sense that it is chosen arbitrarily, it can be regarded as artificial. Certain poets, taking artificiality to be undesirable, attempted to make their language rhythms

146

organic to the meaning of their poems, *free* of abstract metrical forms. What they did in effect was to *spring* the contrapuntal tension between rhythm and meter by removing meter as an *independent* pattern in the poem.

But not many poets have wished in practice to unburden themselves entirely of abstract forms. The difference between free verse and other verse does not, really, lie in the presence or absence of abstract form, but rather in the dependability with which it occurs: in "obligated," traditional verse, form is largely *predictable*; in "free" verse, it is *retrospective* (seen only after being read) and uncommitted, the poet feeling free to shift from one pattern to another at any time. Indeed, even the freest verse *can* be described as a freely varied mixture of feet or lines, but there is rarely any point in doing so. In conventional verse, we are surprised when the meter is discontinued; in free verse, we are surprised when it is continued. But both kinds can exploit rhythmical organization.

So the best general definition of free verse might be *poetry not containing predictable abstract forms*. This allows room for both the kind of poetry where no recognizable structures appear and the kind where structure may appear, but does so without guarantee. In the former, the shape of the lines is thought of as unique and an organic relationship to the content is thought of as replacing objective structures. The second kind uses a combination of structures or partial structures in a variety of ways, and is what we are concerned with here. It can be described as *poetry where the abstract form is retrospective*. Some of the main types of this verse may be classified as follows.

PROSE-POETRY

Poetry has humorously been defined as language printed in lines that stop short of the right-hand margin. Prose-poetry can be defined, accordingly, as poetry printed in lines that extend to the right-hand margin.

It may be useful to distinguish between the physical existence of words, audially and visually, and the meanings and relationships they represent. When words become poetry, their physical properties become as important as their meanings. **Prose-poetry** is language that looks like prose on the printed page, but that is dedicated to being itself as much as to communicating something else. We often find in it a strong repetition or parallelism of consonants, vowels, phrases, images, fragments of rhythm, and so on. The term **polyphonic prose** has been applied to prose that is free to use the resources of poetry, including rhyme, meter, and assonance. Thus it is possible for a paragraph to exploit poetic techniques and still be considered prose, while a paragraph using none of these will be considered poetry. It all depends on the person doing the considering.

Here are some examples of prose-poetry (or poetic prose):

> It is night; I am alone, forlorn on the hill of storms. The wind is heard in the mountain. The torrent pours down the rock. No hut receives me from the rain; forlorn on the hill of winds!

(Note the recurrence of sounds, words, and phrases.)

> Go thy way, eat thy bread with joy, and drink thy wine with a merry heart; for God now accepteth thy works.
>
> Let thy garments be always white; and let thy head lack no ointment.
>
> Live joyfully with the wife whom thou lovest all the days of the life of thy vanity, which he hath given thee under the sun, all the days of thy vanity: for that is thy portion in this life, and in thy labour which thou takest under the sun.
>
> Whatsoever thy hand findeth to do, do it with thy might; for there is no work, nor device, nor knowledge, nor wisdom, in the grave, whither thou goest.
>
> I returned, and saw under the sun, that the race is not to the swift, nor the battle to the strong, neither yet bread to the wise, nor yet riches to men of understanding, nor yet favour to men of skill; but time and chance happeneth to them all.

By degrees we beheld the infinite Abyss, fiery as the smoke
of a burning city; beneath us, at an immense distance, was the
sun, black but shining; round it were fiery tracks on which
revolv'd vast spiders, crawling after their prey, which flew, or
rather swum, in the infinite deep, in the most terrific shapes of
animals sprung from corruption; & the air was full of them, &
seem'd composed of them: these are Devils, and are called
Powers of the air. I now asked my companion which was my
eternal lot? he said: "between the black & white spiders."

PHRASAL FREE VERSE

A common feature of free verse is the repetition or echoing
of phrases or words. This sometimes becomes dominant in
the structure of the poem:

And indeed there will be time
For the yellow smoke that slides along the street,
Rubbing its back upon the window-panes;
There will be time, there will be time
To prepare a face to meet the faces that you meet;
There will be time to murder and create,
And time for all the works and days of hands
That lift and drop a question on your plate;
Time for you and time for me,
And time yet for a hundred indecisions,
And for a hundred visions and revisions,
Before the taking of a toast and tea.

Here the "there will be time" element unites the various
phrases with which it is associated, and thereby builds up a
cumulative effect of situation, tone, meaning, and atmosphere. When, in our judgment, the repetition of phrases
serves generally to fill in, solidify, and enlarge upon a central
effect, we may call it **cumulative repetition**. Sometimes,
however, the repeated phrase is followed each time by a new
piece of information or some other element that adds a little
bit to the meaning and extends it farther. This may happen

from one stanza, line, or phrase to another. When we judge
the repetition to be extending the meaning as well as enlarging
upon it, we may call it **incremental repetition**:

> She put her hand to the nail, and her right hand to the
> workmen's hammer; and with the hammer she smote Sisera,
> she smote off his head, when she had pierced and stricken
> through his temples. At her feet he bowed, he fell, he lay
> down: at her feet he bowed, he fell: where he bowed, there
> he fell down dead.
>
> The mother of Sisera looked out at a window, and cried
> through the lattice, Why is his chariot so long in coming? why
> tarry the wheels of his chariots? Her wise ladies answered her,
> yea, she returned answer to herself, Have they not sped? have
> they not divided the prey; to every man a damsel or two; to
> Sisera a prey of divers colours, a prey of divers colours of
> needlework, of divers colours of needlework on both sides,
> meet for the necks of them that take the spoil?

The systematic repetition of phrases at the beginning of
successive lines is called **anaphora**:

> None has understood you, but I understand you,
> None has done justice to you, you have not done justice to
>   yourself,
> None but has found you imperfect, I only find no imperfection
>   in you,
> None but would subordinate you, I only am he who will never
>   consent to subordinate you.

The difference between cumulative and incremental repetition
is one of convenience only, and in many cases is pointless. We
need not decide whether the meaning is "solidified" or
"extended" in the passage:

> Each of us inevitable,
> Each of us limitless—each of us with his or her right upon the earth,
> Each of us allow'd the eternal purports of the earth,
> Each of us here as divinely as any is here.

SYNTACTIC FREE VERSE

Sometimes the repetitive element in free verse is not the actual words but the syntactic patterns. Words indicating logical relationships (such as prepositions) may recur, but the main impression of form is created when the relationships themselves are repeated through overt or implied parallelisms of syntax:

> The inner freedom from the practical desire,
> The release from action and suffering, release from the inner
> And the outer compulsion, yet surrounded
> By a grace of sense, a white light still and moving,
> *Erhebung* without motion, concentration
> Without elimination, both a new world
> And the old made explicit, understood
> In the completion of its partial ecstasy,
> The resolution of its partial horror.

This passage contains three main clusters of parallel units, which we can indicate by drawing lines as follows:

(1)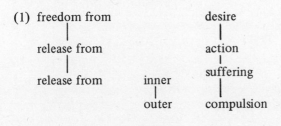

(2)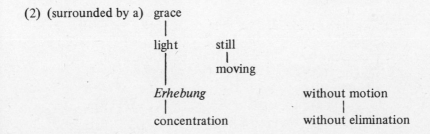

(3) a new (world)
     |
     the old   made explicit
                    |
                    understood   (in) completion of its partial ecstasy
                                    |
                                    resolution of its partial horror.

More commonly, syntactic parallelism is accompanied by phrasal repetition:

> Internal darkness, deprivation
> And destitution of all property,
> Desiccation of the world of sense,
> Evacuation of the world of fancy,
> Inoperancy of the world of spirit.

In this passage, the phrasal repetition is "of the world of" and the syntactic parallelism can be indicated:

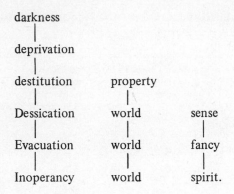

Syntactic or phrasal parallelisms may occur at the beginning, middle, or end of the line, or at no fixed position. Here is a passage where the lines begin with syntactic parallelism and anaphora, and end with phrasal repetition:

> The song is to the singer, and comes back most to him,
> The teaching is to the teacher, and comes back most to him,

The murder is to the murderer, and comes back most to him,
The theft is to the thief, and comes back most to him,
The love is to the lover, and comes back most to him,
The gift is to the giver, and comes back most to him—it cannot fail,
The oration is to the orator, the acting is to the actor and actress
    not to the audience,
And no man understands any greatness or goodness but his own,
    or the indication of his own.

And here is a passage where the syntactic parallelisms, coming at no fixed position, are tied together at the conclusion:

To communicate with Mars, converse with spirits,
To report the behaviour of the sea monster,
Describe the horoscope, haruspicate or scry,
Observe disease in signatures, evoke
Biography from the wrinkles of the palm
And tragedy from fingers; release omens
By sortilege, or tea leaves, riddle the inevitable
With playing cards, fiddle with pentagrams
Or barbituric acids, or dissect
The recurrent image into pre-conscious terrors—
To explore the womb, or tomb, or dreams; all these are usual
Pastimes and drugs, and features of the press.

(This passage has a good deal of enjambment, whereas the one before it is entirely estopped.)

FRAGMENTED FREE VERSE

It is sometimes convenient to think of free verse as containing fragments of various traditional meters. (The passage above, for example, has a few decasyllabic lines, some possible iambic pentameters, and a variety of possible four-stress lines). Alternatively, one can think of free verse as drifting in and out of recognizable metrical patterns, even to the point of using them as *motifs*. Indeed, free verse has been defined as poetry in which the poet is free to use *meter* as he wishes. The scansion given for the following passage is only one of several possibilities, since there is no definitely fixed norm:

The magic car no longer moved.	*iamb. tetram.*
The Fairy and the Spirit	*3s*
Entered the Hall of Spells.	*iamb. trim.*
Those golden clouds	*iamb. dim.*
That rolled in glittering billows	*3s*
Beneath the azure canopy	*iamb. tetram.*
With the ethereal footsteps trembled not;	*iamb. pent.*
The light and crimson mists,	*iamb. trim.*
Floating to strains of thrilling melody	*iamb. pent.*
Through that unearthly dwelling,	*3s*
Yielded to every movement of the will;	*iamb. pent.*
Upon their passive swell the Spirit leaned,	*iamb. pent.*
And, for the varied bliss that pressed around,	*iamb. pent.*
Used not the glorious privilege	*3s*
Of virtue and of wisdom.	*3s*

CADENCED FREE VERSE

Cadenced free verse (CFV) is a term applied to poetry in which *rhythms* are loosely gathered according to the syntactic *phrases* that contain them. The groups of rhythms are seen as having some arrangement, in the way that flowers in a bowl are said to be "arranged," although they are not strictly organized according to a fixed principle.

The smallest rhythmic grouping is the *reading time unit* or **cadence**, defined as the rhythmic shape of the span of language between natural voice pauses (not metrical pauses), measured or described impressionistically. One or more cadences compose a *line*, which is usually estopped; the line as a whole has its **line cadence**. Groups of cadences combine into larger rhythmic patterns called **strophes**, which may differ from each other in tone, atmosphere, and general impression. The strophes in turn may be grouped into stanzas or, more properly, paragraphs (at times identical with strophes), which have their own characters, like the movements of a symphony. The collected strophes of the poem make up the overall rhythmic pattern, which is regarded as organic to that particular poem and therefore unique.

The rhythms of cadenced free verse are meant to be those of ordinary speech. They avoid, theoretically, any contrast between natural and stylized pronunciation, although actually they tend toward the rhetorical and incantatory. It is good to remember that the concept and terminology of cadenced free verse derive from a certain kind of impression of poetry rather than from a certain kind of poetry. The most nearly objective thing we can say about it is that "batches" of rhythms are the most explicit elements of rhythmic organization in it.

All verse is of course cadenced. But in traditional forms the recurrent feature is a metrical pattern, whereas in CFV the recurrence is not so much of actual rhythmic groupings as of general *kinds* of rhythmic groupings, identified partly in terms of whether they are long or short, duple, triple, duple-triple or quadruple, rising, falling or choriambic, pyrrhic or spondaic, etc., and partly in terms of the reader's own notion of rhythmic similarity.

Any cadence is said to have a rhythmic **curve**. When the rhythmic pattern is for some reason clearly identifiable, or becomes quickly familiar, the cadence is said to have a short, tight, or sharp curve; when it is relatively featureless and miscellaneous, as in prose, the cadence is said to have a long or slight curve. One way cadenced free verse differs from ordinary prose is that its rhythmic curve is much shorter, and returns much more sharply upon itself, the **return** being a recurrence of general rhythmic characteristics that causes the reader to associate a given cadence with another that he deems similar.

Generally, the curve of prose-poetry is long. Cadenced free verse "arranges" shorter curves into unrestricted patterns and is free to drift from fragments of meter to the loosest prose rhythms.

Any scansion of CFV is useful mainly to indicate the reader's subjective view of the shape of the rhythms. The following example gives one of many possible scansions. The letters indicate cadences; repeated letters indicate cadences deemed in some way similar, thus creating returns; and the marks # indicate the boundaries of strophes. This example gives two paragraphs out of the poem's seven:

_A Underneath the fallen blossom

_B In my bosom

A Is a letter I have hid.#

A It was brought to me this morning by a rider from the Duke.#
|A

_C "Madam, we regret to inform you that Lord Hartwell

_D Died in action Thursday se'nnight."

_E As I read it in the white, morning sunlight,

A The letters squirmed like snakes.#

_F "Any answer, Madam," said my footman.

_B "No," I told him.

_G "See that the messenger takes some refreshment.

B No, no answer."#

A And I walked into the garden,

D Up and down the patterned paths,

A In my stiff, correct brocade. #

A The blue and yellow flowers stood up proudly in the sun, #
|*D*

B Each one.

D I stood upright too,

A Held rigid to the pattern

A By the stiffness of my gown;

D Up and down I walked,

B Up and down. #

H In a month he would have been my husband.

H In a month, here, underneath this lime,

I We would have broke the pattern; #

J He for me, and I for him,

J He as Colonel, I as Lady, #

~K~ On this shady seat.

~B~ He had a whim

~L~ That sunlight carried blessing. #

~M~ And I answered, "It shall be as you have said."

~B~ Now he is dead. #

This particular scansion happens to divide the first paragraph into seven strophes and the second into four. The cadences happen to be distributed as follows:

paragraph	strophe	cadences	new cadences	number of cadences per strophe
I.	1	A B A	A B	3
	2	A A	– –	2
	3	C D E A	C D E	4
	4	F B G B	F G	4
	5	A D A	– –	3
	6	A D	– –	2
	7	B D A A D B	– –	6
II.	8	H H I	H I	3
	9	J J	J	2
	10	K B L	K L	3
	11	M B	M	2

The two paragraphs in this reading are structurally distinct. In the first one the *progression* is rather *circular*, with the A and B cadences returning (only the fourth strophe lacks an A cadence) and mixing with new cadences. The pattern of the total number of cadences per strophe can be diagramed

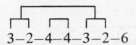

3–2–4–4–3–2–6

showing an orderly balance in the first six strophes. The seventh, which concludes the paragraph, is unusually long, but its cadences create their *own* balanced pattern:

B D A A D B

The second paragraph has four strophes, with a balanced distribution of cadences in a 3–2–3–2 pattern. Each strophe contains at least one new cadence, so that the progression of cadences here is not circular but *sequential*. The only exception to this progress is the B cadence, which concludes *both* paragraphs. One interpretation of these progressions might be that the more circular first section is less clearly developed, picking up threads previously let go, while the second section has a clearer, straighter, but ultimately more surprising development, moving directly ahead but suddenly finding itself back at the earlier B cadence.

It cannot be emphasized too much that this sort of scansion depends almost entirely on individual interpretation. One might, for example, regard the H–H cadences of Paragraph II as returns of the C–D cadences of Paragraph I; or one might wish to see the passage in terms of full-lines, half-lines, and quarter-lines; or one might adopt a mathematically precise way of classifying cadences. The scansion of cadenced free verse is designed not for objective accuracy, but for communicating the reader's perception and interpretation of fluid forms.

At times the strophes of free verse are quite distinct, clearly separated by paragraphing, and sharply contrasted:

> I don't know how he came,
> shambling, dark, and strong.
>
> He stood in the city and told men:
> My people are fools, my people are young and strong, my people
>   must learn, my people are terrible workers and fighters.
> Always he kept on asking: Where did that blood come from?
>
> They said: You for the fool killer,
>   you for the booby hatch
>   and a necktie party.

In summary, the patterns in this form of free verse are based on the cadences, which in turn are based on the syntactic and logical divisions of meaning. Thus the form grows organically out of content.

ACCENTUAL FREE VERSE (PRIMARY-STRESS VERSE: PSV)

In **accentual free verse** a distinction must be made between primary and secondary levels of stress. Only the primary (or major) stresses are considered part of the structure, the frame upon which the full, varying rhythms are placed. The secondary stresses, like the tertiary and weak ones, are metrically unimportant. The result is a poetry in which the total length of the line varies considerably, while the number of primary stresses often remains fairly constant. Thus, even though accentual free verse shares with ordinary stress-verse a tendency toward ambiguity, a scansion restricted to primary

stresses is sometimes more stable than one using both primaries and secondaries:

	stresses		
	secondary	*total*	*primary*
Thőugh my ríme be rãgged,	1	3	2
Tãttered and jãgged,	0	2	2
Rűdely rãine-béaten,	1	3	2
Rűsty and mőth-éaten;	1	3	2
Íf ye tãke wĕl therewíth,	2	4	2
It hãth in ít some píth.	1	3	2

It is sometimes difficult, sometimes impossible, and sometimes unnecessary to maintain a distinction between "stresses"
and "primary stresses." But when that distinction is useful
as in the scansion of some accentual free verse, it must be
based on natural speech rhythms, uninfluenced by the visual
grouping of words into lines.

Primary-stress verse may, instead of holding to a fixed
number of stresses per line, establish certain *limits* within
which the stress-count varies:

primary stresses

To a Snail

If "compréssion is the first grace of style,"	3
you have it. Contractílity is a vírtue	3
as módesty is a vírtue.	2
It is nót the acquisítion of any one thíng	3

primary stresses

that is áble to adórn,	2
or the incidéntal quálity that occúrs	3
as a concómitant of sómething well sáid,	3
that we válue in stýle,	2
but the prínciple that is híd:	2
in the ábsence of féet, "a méthod of conclúsions";	4
"a knówledge of prínciples,"	2
in the cúrious phenómenon of your occípital hórn.	4

The "pattern" created by this stress-count can be described in many ways. One possible division is into three sections, the first and third echoing each other and separated by a brace of 3's:

$$3-3-2-3-2$$
$$3-3$$
$$2-2-4-2-4$$

We can represent the relationships in the first section as A–A–B–A–B. But this is also the pattern of the last section, where the 2's have moved from B-position to A-position and 4's have come into B-position.

There is nothing conclusive about any of this. We can set up a structure less abstract and more organic by dividing according to the syntax, and this will yield the pattern 3–3–2, 3–2, 3–3–2, 2–4–2–4. The numerical relationships may then be represented A–A–B, A–B, A–A–B, $\begin{Bmatrix} B-C-B-C \\ \text{or} \\ A-B-A-B \end{Bmatrix}$, three *progressive* or *developmental* relationships followed by a final *alternating* or *interlocking* one. The point is not to find *the* pattern but to be aware that *a* pattern can be found in the poem.

Primary-stress verse is capable of a kind of flowing smoothness not easily achieved in more restricted forms. Here is a

passage where we may hear three or four or five stresses per
line, depending on the level we listen to:

PSV 4s:

> If we áll were júdged accórding to the cónsequences
> Of áll our words and déeds, beyónd the inténtion
> And beyónd our límited understánding   *3ps*
> Of oursélves and óthers, we should áll be condémned.
> Mrs. Chámberlayne, I óften have to máke a decísion
> Which may méan restorátion or rúin to a pátient—
> And sómetimes I have máde the wróng decísion.
> As for Miss Cóplestone, becáuse you think her déath was wáste
> You bláme yoursélves, and becáuse you blame yoursélves
> You thínk her lífe was wásted. It was triúmphant.
> But I am nó more respónsible for the tríumph—   *3ps*
> And júst as respónsible for her déath as yóu are.

CHAPTER VII
USING THE SCANSION

To the question "What do we *do* with a scansion once we have made it?" a legitimate answer is "We brood over it," or "We look at it, we contemplate it." To the much more frequent question "Why bother to scan the meter of a poem at all?" the answers are many; but we do poetry a disservice if we fail to recognize that a single response ought to be sufficient: "Because the rhythms we describe are one of the activities going on in the poem." If we do not see the rhythmic structure, we simply do not see the entire poem. "Why bother to organize our impressions of the rhythms?" is equivalent to "Why bother to organize our impressions of the ideas, perceptions, philosophies, images, symbols, allusions, rhetorical devices, and traditions in the poem?" The understanding of rhythmic structures requires no more apology for poetry than for music.

Meter (that is, the scansion we arrive at) is our statement about a poem. It is a statement, an abstract idea like a common denominator in a series of fractions, that summarizes the tendencies of the rhythms. It is an outline, a tool for organizing and defining. We scan the words to see how best to describe the way the rhythms are combined and perhaps organized into patterns, and that is why our kind of metrical study is properly called *scansion*: it is inductive rather than deductive, descriptive rather than prescriptive. The metrical rules we formulate as the result of our scansions can be strict or loose, and the poems to which we apply them can follow them strictly or loosely or can break them outright.

Scansions are not right or wrong but rather illuminating or confusing. One man's trochaic trimeter with anacrusis is another's iambic trimeter hypercatalectic and yet another's three-stress duple and yet another's Half Measure and yet another's heptasyllabic, all depending on their point and their frame of reference. Any system of metrical analysis is largely arbitrary in principle and terminology.

The abstract goal in learning scansion is development of a capacity for the appreciation of a certain kind of form. The concrete goal is development of an ear for the rhythms moving through the poem: by learning to put labels on metrical features we learn to hear rhythmic effects more acutely. By setting up some fixed metrical pattern, we can use it as an abstract frame of reference against which to measure—and thereby to experience with more understanding—the actual rhythms of poems.

The form of any specific scansion is not usually as important as the knowledge it gives that the rhythms are—or can be—organized in some describable pattern. But this cannot be demonstrated unless we actually commit ourselves to a specific scansion. So scansion is a means by which we solidify or objectify our sense of form or shape within the verbal sequence.

In following rules and principles, in embodying traditions and conventions, scansion gives us a point of juncture between fixed and variable elements. It is another means by which we see the poet drawing energy from the opposition of traditional and unique, public and private, theoretic and actual, abstract and concrete, and the fixed and the developing.

Scansion gives the poem texture and physicality for us. It directs our attention to the real presence of the poem as an actual verbal object or immediate event, and so it helps to prevent us from thinking of poetry only in terms of *meaning*, as though poems were merely casings for more important substances. In any art, as the saying goes, form is as much a part of the meaning as content is.

By making us conscious of metrical organization, then, scansion brings to the surface three main kinds of relationships: first, between the rhythmic pulsations we respond to physiologically and the sophisticated mathematical arrangements we understand intellectually; this is the interpenetration of physical acoustic events and abstract ideas, where actual rhythms are given greater "meaning" from belonging to a pattern and where ideal patterns are given greater "immediacy" by being incarnated into sounds. Secondly, there is the inter-penetration of spontaneous exuberance (as represented by rhythmic variations) and predictable control (the metrical norm). Thirdly, there is the interpenetration of the unpredictable development of word-meanings and the steady dependability provided by metrical pattern.

By learning the language of scansion we acquire another way of talking about poems. It is a language that serves fairly well to convey our perceptions with originality and objectivity. As a method of classification, it economically points up differences and similarities, enabling us to compare words, passages, poems, poets, traditions, or esthetic theories.

Scansion helps us appreciate the meaning and esthetics of variation. When we know that a rule is being broken or amended we become more aware of rules generally, especially if we discover that the variations themselves follow rules. Form and variation are inseparable and have to be defined in terms of each other. Scansion allows us to see variation as the bridge between theoretic form and actual structure, and it thereby calls attention to the particularizing *texture* that structure gives to form. It makes us aware of variation as a purely musical thing: variation for the *sake* of form. And it illuminates some of the kinds of counterpoint available to the poet.

Thus, although scansion is able to contrast the meter with the word-boundaries, syllable-counts, and cadences, its main function is to record the difference between meter and rhythm. The process may be summarized by an example.

(1) We know that the iambic pentameter norm requires the rhythm of a line to be arranged metrically in the pattern:

$$x - | x - | x - | x - | x -$$

(2) In an iambic pentameter context we encounter:

When I consider how my light is spent.

This line can be "performed" in different ways, one typical rhythmic pattern being:

− x x − x x x − x −

(3) The scansion, though it might seem rhythmically clumsy and metrically inaccurate, is nevertheless able to convey an implication of both, allowing the critic to indicate his ideas both of meter and of performance. The scansion might be:

− x | x − | x ⌄ | x − | x −

There has been a compromise. The scansion indicates the performer's rhythmic preference for stressing the first syllable more than the second and for reading the sixth syllable as weaker than the first, fourth, eighth, and tenth. But it also demonstrates that the line, a jagged four-stresser in duple-triple-quadruple rhythm, qualifies metrically as iambic pentameter, using only the variations standard in that form. This double function can be diagramed (using another example) as follows:

Of Mans First Disobedience, and the Fruit

x	−	−	x	x −	x x	x	x	−	*rhythm*
x	−	−	x	x −	x̆	⌄	x	−	**scansion** (compromise)
x	−	x	−	x −	x	−	x	−	*meter*

Scansion can relate the structure of a poem to its logical meaning. This is not to say that meters in themselves contain any sort of meaning, emotion, or mood; to speak of gay meters or dignified meters or ominous meters is to miss the entire point. Meter works in partnership with meaning. We sometimes have the impression that the meter or rhythm is exactly conveying what the words also are conveying, in a kind of rhythmic onomatopoeia. But it is an illusion, a desirable one. The logical content and the meter harmonize or dance a duet, and it is the combined motion that makes us think they are saying the same thing. We turn two impressions into one observation, just as our eyes combine two two-dimensional perceptions into a single one of three dimensions or as we fuse sights and sounds into single experiences, as though our different senses were getting the same information. In its own dimension, moreover, the meter can create disturbances or special effects, making us pay particular attention to a particular section of the poem and thus causing us to be more receptive to any special effects in the meaning as well.

The meter-meaning relationship is brought out by metrical analysis, which may vary from the quantitative to the freely interpretive. A passage where meter and meaning seem closely related therefore provides a good opportunity for illustrating some of the ways scansion can be used. Let us consider the first scene of Shakespeare's *King Lear.*

In this scene Lear renounces both the throne of England and the one daughter who truly loves him. He is able to succeed in committing these two errors because, as king, he will not suffer criticism or interference. Lear's majesty is part of his weakness; he is egotistical, rash, and unaware of any world other than the one that is supposed to revolve around him. He insists on the formulas of courtly decorum, while his language, when angry, betrays his mind as seething with anguish and hatred. These qualities come to the surface more often as, in the course of the play, the denial of his kingly prerogatives increasingly fills his speech with images of disease, impotence, and sterility, rising perhaps out of disappointment at having produced no male heir to the throne.

The play begins in prose, with some gentlemen discussing Lear's abdication and other matters. Then Lear enters, with his royal train, announced by fanfare. After giving some instructions, Lear delivers his first speech, and it is a respectable blank verse:

LEAR. Meantime we shall express our darker purpose.
Give me that map there. Know that we have divided
In three our kingdom. And 'tis our fast intent
To shake all cares and business from our age,
Conferring them on younger strengths while we
Unburdened crawl toward death. Our son of Cornwall,
And you, our no less loving son of Albany . . .

The iambic pentameter is orderly but not constrained, with
an awareness of medial cesuras on the one hand and a frequent
allowance of feminine endings on the other. Although Lear
enjoys his own oratory and frequently indulges himself in it,
he is here merely being correct and transacting business of
state. We ought, however, to notice the way in which he
expresses himself as crawling toward death, a dramatized bit
of self-indulgence which, although perhaps reflecting some
fears—possibly about a heart condition—is contrasted with the
fact that he still rides out to hunt.

The time has come for the announcement of the division of
the kingdom into three portions, to be dowries for Lear's
three daughters, Goneril, Regan, and Cordelia. Partly for
ceremoniousness and partly to gratify his appetite for flattery,
Lear asks his daughters to tell him, each in turn, how much
they love him, with the pretense that the winning contestant
will receive the best portion of the kingdom. Goneril, the
eldest, speaks first:

GONERIL. Sir, I love you more than words can wield the
    matter,
Dearer than eyesight, space, and liberty,
Beyond what can be valued, rich or rare,
No less than life, with grace, health, beauty, honor,
As much as child e'er loved or father found—
A love that makes breath poor and speech unable—
Beyond all manner of so much I love you.

A competent pentameter for a princess, including the sequence
"grace, health, beauty, honor," two monosyllabic nouns

followed by two disyllabic nouns in falling rhythm, where "health" must be demoted to slack, leaving grace, beauty, and honor the main qualities of a good life. The first line of the speech may be interpreted in several ways. It has six stresses instead of five, understandable in the light of Goneril's apparent enthusiasm. But this is not exactly the alexandrine that blank verse sometimes uses, because alexandrines are iambic hexameter while this line is *trochaic* hexameter, six feet in perfect falling rhythm. However, we need not fear a violation of tradition: words of address are sometimes hypermetric, not to be counted in the scansion. Thus if we ignore the "Sir" we have a simple iambic pentameter with feminine ending.

Lear turns to the map of the kingdom and assigns Goneril her portion of land without having heard the other daughters. He then asks a tribute of love from Regan, who replies:

> *REGAN.* I am made of that self metal as my sister,
> And prize me at her worth. In my true heart
> I find she names my very deed of love,
> Only she comes too short. That I profess
> Myself an enemy to all other joys
> Which the most precious square of sense possesses,
> And find I am alone felicitate
> In your dear Highness' love.

Regan, unoriginal and not quite so accomplished as her older sister, builds upon what Goneril invents. She echoes Goneril's professions of love and then tries to outdo them by treacherously implying that Goneril was merely speaking *words*. But in attempting to imitate Goneril's initial trochaic hexameter, Regan does not realize that the first stress is meant to be hypermetric: in her speech, the first word is not a word of address and cannot be removed, and so she is stuck with a line of six trochees. Having had the advantage of going second, however, she manages to outdo Goneril's performance at least a little: Goneril's speech is seven lines long; Regan's is seven and three-fifths.

Rewarding Regan with an "ample third" of the kingdom,
Lear then turns to the youngest, his favorite, Cordelia. What
can she tell him of her love for him?

CORDELIA. Nothing, my lord.

Cordelia's answer is two-fifths of a line, four syllables. Lear
is left speechless, or almost so, for he cannot conceive the
meaning or even accept the reality of Cordelia's reply. There
must be a mistake; otherwise the outrage to himself would be
insupportable. He would like to erase the event, have his
youngest daughter try again, so he gives her one more
chance—three more, actually—to pay her tribute:

90   *LEAR.* Nothing!

91   *CORDELIA.* Nothing.

92   *LEAR.* Nothing will come of nothing. Speak again.

93   *CORDELIA.* Unhappy that I am, I cannot heave

94   My heart into my mouth. I love your Majesty

95   According to my bond, nor more nor less.

96   *LEAR.* How, how, Cordelia! Mend your speech a little,

97   Lest it may mar your fortunes.

      CORDELIA.   Good my lord,

98   You have begot me, bred me, loved me. I

99   Return those duties back as are right fit,

100   Obey you, love you, and most honor you.

101   Why have my sisters husbands if they say

102   They love you all? Haply, when I shall wed,

103   That lord whose hand must take my plight shall carry

104   Half my love with him, half my care and duty.

105   Sure, I shall never marry like my sisters,

106   To love my father all.

107   *LEAR.* But goes thy heart with this?

     CORDELIA.   Aye, good my lord.

108   *LEAR.* So young, and so untender?

109   *CORDELIA.* So young, my lord, and true.

110   *LEAR.* Let it be so. Thy truth then be thy dower.

111   For, by the sacred radiance of the sun,

112   The mysteries of Hecate, and the night,

113   By all the operation of the orbs

114   From whom we do exist and cease to be,

115   Here I disclaim all my paternal care,

116   Propinquity, and property of blood,

117   And as a stranger to my heart and me

118   Hold thee from this forever. The barbarous Scythian,

119   Or he that makes his generation messes

120   To gorge his appetite shall to my bosom

121   Be as well neighbored, pitied, and relieved

122   As thou my sometime daughter.

     KENT.   Good my liege—

     LEAR. Peace, Kent!

123   Come not between the dragon and his wrath.

124   I loved her most, and thought to set my rest

125   On her kind nursery. Hence, and avoid my sight!

126   So be my grave my peace, as here I give

127   Her father's heart from her! Call France. Who stirs?

128   Call Burgundy. Cornwall and Albany,

129   With my two daughters' dowers digest this third.

130   Let pride, which she calls plainness, marry her.

In this scene Lear moves from astonishment to a sweeping fury that mingles images of the "kind nursery" he has apparently lost with images of monstrosities.

We know that in drama one speech may end with a section of a line that will be completed by the opening section of the following speech, usually in a stress-pattern of 3 + 2 or 2 + 3. But the exchange of "nothings" between Lear and Cordelia does not link in this way; we have simply awkward line fragments until Lear uses the word twice at line 92 and restores the pentameter. Cordelia then achieves the pentameter herself, but with language that is labored and inadequate, requiring promotions and including a light ending at line 94. Lear again threatens and encourages, and then breaks off at line 97, creating a feminine cesura after the third foot, asking Cordelia to "mend" her speech. Cordelia picks up the meter to complete a faultless pentameter line (with first foot inverted) and then proceeds to make one of her fullest speeches in the play, devoid of ornamentation but honest, direct, and throwing a cold light upon the posturings of her sisters. This time it is Lear who cannot reply properly: at line 107 he follows her three-foot line with another three-footer instead of the required two-footer.

By this time we may have become aware of another feature of Cordelia's speech. She twice uses syntactic units of *three*, in the phrases "begot me, bred me, loved me" and "obey you,

love you, and most honor you." This three-unit tendency is
far more evident in the *cadences* of her speech:

> Unháppy thát I ám
> According to my bond
> Begot me, bred me, loved me
> Return those duties back
> Haply, when I shall wed
> Half my care and duty
> To love my father all
> Aye, good my lord
> So young, my lord, and true

The presence of so many three-foot sections may be explained
by Cordelia's tendency to speak in shorter phrases than the
others. Her speeches frequently have medial cesuras, which
would make either the first or the second section of a line a
three-footer. Whatever the cause, a strong three-stress cross-
rhythm runs through her language in a kind of opposition to
the more expansive pentameters of her father. Lear's own
speeches contain a good many medial cesuras, but as his
passion grows so also do the lengths of his cadences.

   At lines 107 ff. Lear and Cordelia again fail to link their
line fragments into full lines, both repeating three-foot sections, until Lear says "Let it be so," a phrase pivotal both
thematically and metrically. Let us rearrange the passage:

106	*CORDELIA.*		To love my father all.
107a	*LEAR.*		But goes thy heart with this?
107b	*CORDELIA.*		Aye, good my lord.
108	*LEAR.*		So young, and so untender?
109	*CORDELIA.*		So young, my lord, and true.
110	*LEAR.*	Let it be so.	Thy truth then be thy dower.

Here we have, in effect, a **stichomythia** or single-line dialogue made of trimeters, or rather of three-stress lines since at 107b Cordelia moves into stress-verse. The phrase "Let it be so" is pivotal because in it Lear, making his wrong decision, turns from his daughter and moves back into the world of majesty and incipient panic that he has created for himself. The phrase "Thy truth then be thy dower" is the metrical bridge between the two worlds. In itself it exactly parallels the scansion of line 108, and the line that intervenes, spoken by Cordelia, differs only by a masculine ending:

108   So young, and so untender?   x — | x — | x — | x

109   So young, my lord, and true.   x — | x — | x — |

110   Thy truth then be thy dower.   x — | x — | x — | x

But when we add to this pattern the *first* section of line 110, the pivotal line becomes a normal pentameter. Thus line 110 belongs to the concluding part of the three-stress father-daughter dialogue and also to the beginning part of the sweeping royal pentameters:

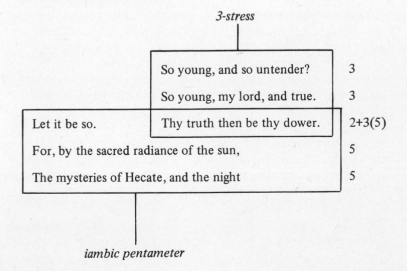

	3-stress	
	So young, and so untender?	3
	So young, my lord, and true.	3
Let it be so.	Thy truth then be thy dower.	2+3(5)
For, by the sacred radiance of the sun,		5
The mysteries of Hecate, and the night		5

iambic pentameter

Line 111 begins the oath whereby Lear abdicates his responsibilities as a father (a decision made irrevocable by the traumatic images of cannibalism) and so disqualifies himself from receiving any daughter's love, which, if it comes, must now come as an act of grace, not duty. In uttering the terrible words he uses a diction and syntax that are formal, ostentatious, ritualistic, stylized, incantatory, involuted, and impersonal. The subject of the first long sentence is "I," the verb is "disclaim," and the object is "paternal care." But we notice that it is really a double sentence, the main content of which is "I disclaim my paternal care and hold thee from this." The scansion of the passage is:

111 x – | x – | x – | x – | x –

112 x – | x – | x – | x – | x –

113 x – | x – | x – | x – | x –

114 x – | x – | x – | x – | x –

115 [– x] x – [– x] x – | x – ←

116 x – | x – | x – | x – | x –

117 x – | x – | x – | x – | x –

118 [– x] x – | x ≚ | x – | x̆ – | x̆ ←

The unusual thing here is the extreme metrical regularity. Discounting elisions, this entire passage is varied by a feminine ending and only three trochaic inversions (not counting a possible one in the first foot of line 111). Those three trochees form the initial choriambic cadences of the three phrases "Here I disclaim," "all my paternal," and "Hold thee from this." That is, in a field of unusually regular meters, the three disturbances are created at the core of the syntax.

Looking back to the beginning of this speech, we find that line 110 also begins with an inversion: $\dfrac{\text{Let it be so.}}{-\ \text{x}\ |\ \text{x}\ -}$ Thus the choriambic cadences in the first foot of line 110 and the first foot of line 115 make a kind of frame for the material between.

It may help to review the metrical development of this passage. Line 110, we saw, completes the three-stress cadence of the dialogue with Cordelia but also makes a return to the blank verse form, beginning with the characteristic initial inversion. Immediately following this, beginning at line 111, the blank verse pattern is pure, and continues so for four lines, as long as Lear is delaying his subject and verbs with increasingly complex phrases:

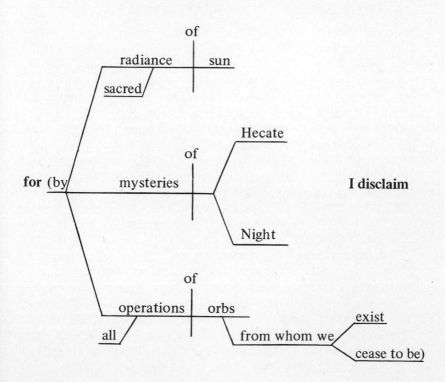

Then, as he announces his disclaimer of moral responsibility, the line is disrupted with one trochee at the beginning and another in the third foot, creating consecutive slacks and stresses at three places,

> Here I disclaim all my paternal care
> — x| x — |— x | x —| x —

where the shock is reinforced by his sudden shift from the royal "we" to the personal "I." This is followed by two more lines in pure blank verse, and the sentence then ends with the second main clause, where we encounter the first feminine ending of the speech and the first of a series:

> Hold thee from this forever. The barbarous Scythian
> — x | x — | x —|(x) ‖ x — | x̆ — | x̆
> | x ≌ ‖

    Line 122 concludes with a section of three feet, completed by the two-stresser of Kent, who wants to intercede on Cordelia's behalf when he sees that Lear's anger has run out of control. But Lear is in a rage. He is king, and he has not finished speaking, or at any rate his vow is not to be capped by an earl. Now if Kent's fragment is taken as completing Lear's line, Lear's reply to Kent amounts to a dimeter variation among the pentameters:

> As thou my sometime daughter. Good my liege—   5
> Peace, Kent!   2
> Come not between the dragon and his wrath.   5

We might conclude that the dimeter is perfectly suited to Lear's rage as an extrametrical cry of anger, or something of that sort. But "Peace, Kent!" is not a dimeter variation; it does not contain two feet; in fact, it contains no slacks at all: it is pure stress-verse. Lear wants no reply, nor will he suffer anyone to complete his meters, so he obliterates Kent's dimeter in the shortest way possible. He *replaces* Kent's two stresses with two of his own, trying to rewrite the dialogue just as he did with Cordelia. With Kent's words annulled, Lear's iambic pentameter remains unbroken:

> Be as well neighbored, pitied, and relieved
> As thou my sometime daughter. Peace, Kent!
> Come not between the dragon and his wrath.

In the last part of the interview, Lear's pentameters break up again into shorter cadences as he summons his people and begins to make arrangements for dividing Cordelia's portion among Goneril and Regan.

There is no need to argue that these metrical effects are consciously used by the characters or painstakingly worked out by Shakespeare. They are not cleverly coded bits of "meaning." But to the degree that we choose to see them, they give depth to our impressions of characters and situations. We come to recognize and to be guided by speech patterns as well as by peculiarities of diction or of ideas.

It may be clearer now why metrical analysis has been an area of dispute for centuries. This is all to the good, so long as the critic is not driven to the belief that his analysis reveals the final, single truth. The most we expect of a critic is that he give us a fresh way of looking at a poem.

APPENDIX 1. COMMON STANZAS

A grouping or "batch" of lines is called a *stanza* or *verse paragraph*. The distinction between the two is not ultimately clear. A stanza repeats some formal (abstract) pattern, and typically comes to an end when the mathematical demands upon it have been met. The verse paragraph is a continuous form, made of single lines unlinked formally to other lines, and gathered into unequal groups of thought, meaning, logic, or content. It comes to an end when the subject changes. The appearance of a poem on the page usually indicates whether the line arrangement is continuous or stanzaic. Groups of two rhymed lines, however, may be printed continuously, building larger groupings in the way single lines do. Consistently rhymed units of three or more lines are usually printed separately and are thought of as stanzaic. There are also ambiguous forms, such as some odes, where the lines are clustered according to the thought and the metrical pattern is not predictable, but where the effect is primarily stanzaic. Some persons reserve the term *stanza* for cases where a formal pattern is repeated; others use it wherever the general impression is more one of the divisions of a song than the divisions of an intellectual argument.

While lines of poetry may be gathered into batches according to meter, typography, punctuation, rhythmic cadence, dominant imagery, argument, and so forth, the gathering in most forms traditional today is done through rhyme, one of the richest and most complex of poetic techniques. There are so many kinds of relationships between sounds that rhyme, no less than meter, is subject to ambiguity and interpretation. To avoid these problems here, we will regard rhyme simply as "a significant linking of sounds." (See Appendix 2.)

Since the number of variations possible in even simple stanzas is huge, we will cover here only some of the most common standard patterns.

Single Lines (unrhymed)

Only one line-length has been fully successful as a continuous form.   This is the unrhymed iambic pentameter, called **blank verse**. Because of its frequent use in English epic or heroic poems it is also called *heroic verse*, a term more strictly reserved, however, for iambic pentameter couplets. Blank verse uses the variations standard in iambic pentameter, sometimes limiting itself to trochaic inversion, feminine ending, modification and alteration; and sometimes more freely allowing modal shift, anacrusis, and epic cesura. Sometimes also it varies the line-length with *short-lines* or *cut lines* (usually iambic dimeter or trimeter) or with *lengthened lines* of iambic hexameter (alexandrine) and on rare occasion even the iambic heptameter (septenary).

The flexibility of blank verse also lends itself to another feature.   When rhythmic cadences are counterpointed with the metrical norm, breaking or joining the pentameter lines through cesuras or enjambment, they create a kind of sub-surface undercurrent called **cross-rhythm**:

Blank verse with primarily 3s cross-rhythm:

	stresses per cross-rhythmic cadence
The Birds thir quire apply; aires, vernal aires,	3
1 2 3 # 1 2 3 #	3
Breathing the smell of field and grove, attune	
1 2 3 4 # 1	4
The trembling leaves, while Universal *Pan*	3
2 3 # 1 2 3 #	3
Knit with the *Graces* and the *Hours* in dance	
1 2 3 4 5 #	5
Led on th' Eternal Spring. Not that faire field	
1 2 3 # 1 2	3

stresses per
cross-rhythmic cadence

Of *Enna,* where *Proserpin* gathring flours   3
   3 #   1   2   3 #   3

Her self a fairer Floure by gloomie *Dis*
   1   2   3 #   1   2   3

Was gatherd, which cost *Ceres* all that pain   3
      3#   1   2   3   4#   4

To seek her through the world.
   1   2   3 #   3

(Notice the submerged 3–3–4–3 Poulter's Measure pattern in the first four and the last four cadences). Cross-rhythms are more common in blank verse than in other forms.

Two other lines have gained some popularity in blank form, though not as much as the iambic pentameter. These are the six-stress line in falling rhythm and the trochaic tetrameter. Non-stanzaic verse with *occasional rhyme,* where only some of the lines are rhymed and in no fixed pattern, can also be regarded as a continuous form.

Two Lines

When iambic pentameter lines are rhymed in pairs they create **heroic verse** (HV) or, less ambiguously, **heroic couplets** (HC). This form allows for some effects not easily achieved in blank arrangements. For example, the relationship between the first and second sections of the first line in the brace may be contrasted, repeated, paralleled, or extended in the second line:

Created half to rise, and half to fall;
————(1a)————‖————(1b)————

Great lord of all things, yet a prey to all.
————(2a)————————‖————(2b)————

Here the balance between "rise" and "fall" is sustained in the balance between "lord" and "prey," and the "rise"/"lord" relationship is echoed in "fall"/"prey." Thus we have both vertical and horizontal linkings.

An important variation in the heroic couplet is the *triplet* rhyme, frequently indicated by a bracket:

Heroic couplets:

For close Designs and crooked Counsels fit,	*a*
Sagacious, Bold, and Turbulent of wit,	*a*
Restless, unfixt in Principles and Place,	*b*
In Pow'r unpleased, impatient of Disgrace;	*b*
A fiery Soul, which working out its way,	*c*
Fretted the Pigmy Body to decay:	*c*
And o'r informed the Tenement of Clay.	*c*
A daring Pilot in extremity;	*d*
Pleas'd with the Danger, when the Waves went high	*d*
He sought the Storms; but, for a Calm unfit,	*e*
Would Steer too nigh the Sands to boast his Wit.	*e*

The third line of a triplet variation is sometimes an alexandrine, and in some poets such a [5] *a a* [6] *a* pattern is found most often at the conclusion of paragraphs or (in drama) of speeches.

The Folk Meters are basically couplets. Poulter's Measure is a couplet of unequal lines, one twelver followed by one fourteener, or HM followed by CM. We also have some six-stress and seven-stress couplets, which can often be regarded as versions of HM or CM. The choice of terminology (e.g., heptameter, septenary, seven-stress, fourteener, Common Measure) depends on the total impression, including degree of syllabic regularity, modal shift, fixed cesuras, pauses, differential, isochronism, dipodism, and so forth.

After the heroic verse and the Folk Meters, the most popular couplet form has been the four-stress, which stays around an octosyllabic norm and is called the **Hudibrastic** or **octosyllabic couplet**:

Octosyllabic couplets:

Beside he was a shrewd *Philosopher,*	*9 syll.*
And had read every Text and gloss over:	*9 syll.*
What e'er the crabbed'st Author hath	
He understood b' implicit Faith,	
What ever *Sceptick* could inquire for;	*9 syll.*
For every *why* he had a *wherefore*;	*9 syll.*
Knew more than forty of them do,	
As far as words and terms could go.	

(All the hypermetric lines here are with feminine ending. The first two lines are redundant even after elision).

Three Lines

The words *triplet* and *tercet* are often used interchangeably to refer to bundles of three lines. Specifically, however, **triplet** applies to stanzas rhyming *a a a, b b b, c c c*, etc., in which each stanza is formally independent:

Octosyllabic (4s) triplets:

He clasps the crag with crooked hands;	*a*
Close to the sun in lonely lands,	*a*
Ringed with the azure world, he stands.	*a*

The wrinkled sea beneath him crawls;	*b*
He watches from his mountain walls,	*b*
And like a thunderbolt he falls.	*b*

Tercet applies specifically where the middle line of one stanza rhymes with the outer lines of the following stanza, making the scheme *a b a, b c b, c d c, d e d*, etc. When this form is in iambic pentameter, it is **terza rima**:

O wild West Wind, thou breath of Autumn's being,	*a*
Thou, from whose unseen presence the leaves dead	*b*
Are driven, like ghosts from an enchanter fleeing,	*a*
Yellow, and black, and pale, and hectic red,	*b*
Pestilence-stricken multitudes: O thou,	*c*
Who chariotest to their dark wintry bed	*b*
The wingèd seeds, where they lie cold and low,	*c*
Each like a corpse within its grave, until	*d*
Thine azure sister of the Spring shall blow	*c*

Four Lines

The four-line stanza, one of the most popular in English, is short enough to make a tight bundle yet long enough to contain detail and variety. The *x a x a* quatrain (where *x* represents an unrhymed line) apparently comes from the Common Measure couplet broken into hemistichs, and it usually occurs where the stress-pattern is 4—3—4—3. This *x a x a* rhyme-pattern is said to be in **intermittent rhyme**. The quatrain with an *a b a b* pattern is in **alternate** or *interlocking* or *crossed* rhyme. With an *a b b a* pattern it is in **envelope** or *inserted* rhyme.

Quatrains appear in various line lengths, but after the folk line the most common is the iambic pentameter. When the iambic pentameter rhymes alternately *a b a b* it forms the *heroic stanza* or (to avoid confusion with the heroic couplet) the **heroic quatrain**. When it appears in the pattern *a a x a* it forms the **Rubaiyat Stanza**.

One other well-known quatrain is the iambic tetrameter rhyming in envelope *a b b a*, which forms the **In Memoriam Stanza**.

Five Lines

The five-line stanza is most often rhymed *a b a b b* or *a b a a b*.

Common Measure is susceptible to being lengthened from four hemistichs to five in order to delay or suspend the conclusive phrase, so that the usual 4–3–4–3 pattern becomes 4–3–4–<u>4</u>–3. The usual rhyme scheme for this form is *x a b b a*, but if the irregular fourth hemistich is removed it becomes the standard *x a x a* of broken Folk Meter couplets.

The **cinquain** is a special five-line form with a *syllabic* base. The lines consist of 2, 4, 6, 8, 2 syllables respectively and are unrhymed. Cinquains are not really stanzas so much as short poems in themselves.

Six Lines

Of the many six-line stanzas, three have been particularly distinctive:

Venus and Adonis Stanza: iambic pentameter rhyming *a b a b c c.*

Romance Six: sometimes called **rime couée** or **tail-rhyme stanza.** The rhyme is usually *a a b c c b* or *a a b a a b* and the stress-pattern is 4–4–3–4–4–3, usually in constant duple rhythm (making the syllable-count 8–8–6–8–8–6). It can therefore be seen as an extension of Common Meter, even though that may not be its historical source. The basic unit in this stanza is of the three lines [4] *a a* [3] *b* (a couplet plus a tail or cauda), which is doubled, tripled, etc., to form stanzas of six, nine, or more lines, in multiples of three.

Burns Stanza or **Burns Meter:** Here the rhyme is *a a a b a b*, the usual syllable-count 8–8–8–4–8–4, and the fixed stress-pattern 4–4–4–2–4–2. The first two-stress line in the stanza is the *waist* and the final two-stresser the *tail*.

The **bob-wheel stanza**, which has no fixed length, is similar to the Burns Stanza. It consists of three unequal parts. The main part, done in the metrical staple and conveying the main text of the stanza, comes first and is called the **frons**. It is followed by one or two very short lines called the *bob-verses* or **bob**. The bob is followed by the *tail*, which is made of one or more lines that are longer than the bob but usually shorter than the frons. The tail is usually linked by rhyme to the bob but not to the frons. If, from stanza to stanza, the tail repeats the same words entirely or in part, it is called a **refrain**. If, however, it changes the words but repeats the metrical pattern, it is called a *bob-wheel* or **wheel**:

	Go and catch a falling star,	*a*
	Get with child a mandrake root,	*b*
frons	Tell me where all past years are,	*a*
	Or who cleft the devil's foot,	*b*
	Teach me to hear mermaids singing,	*c*
	Or to keep off envy's stinging,	*c*
bob	And find	*d*
	What wind	*d*
wheel	Serves to advance an honest mind.	*d*

Seven Lines

Rhyme Royal or **rime royal**: iambic pentameter rhyming *a b a b b c c*. Also called *Chaucer's Seven-line Stanza* or the *Chaucerian Seven*, or the **Troilus Stanza**. When the syntax clearly breaks the stanza logically into the three parts *a b—a b—b c c*, the first two parts are called the **pedes** and the last the **cauda**.

Eight Lines

Octaves: *Octave* may refer to any eight-line stanza or to the *complication* of the Italian sonnet. But in themselves octaves are individual poems, unrhymed, in iambic pentameter.

Monk's Tale Stanza: iambic pentameter *a b a b b c b c*. Also called *Chaucer's Eight-line Stanza* or the *Chaucerian Eight*.

Folk Meter doubled: Folk Meter couplets doubled and broken into hemistichs make eight-line stanzas.

Ottava Rima: ("rhymed octaves"); iambic pentameter *a b a b a b c c.*

Triolet: This poem is more a feat of rhyming than of meter, consisting of a constant metrical norm (such as 3s or 4s lines) with a scheme of *A B a A a b A B*, where capital letters indicate the repetition of the entire line.

Nine Lines

Spenserian Stanza: Eight lines of iambic pentameter followed by a final alexandrine (iambic hexameter). Sometimes described as eight decasyllabics followed by one duodecasyllabic. The rhyme scheme is *a b a b b c b c c.*

When, as here, all the lines in the stanza except the last are metrically identical, that last line is a **clausula.**

Stanza and Poem Forms of More than Nine Lines

Sonnet: The sonnet usually consists of fourteen lines of rhymed iambic pentameter. Two main kinds are popular. The first, known as the **Italian** or **Petrarchan** sonnet, divides the poem into one batch of eight lines and one of six, where the octave rhymes *a b b a   a b b a* and the sestet introduces two or three new rhymes, as *c d   c d   c d* or *c d e   c d e.* The main rhyming division between octave and sestet is paralleled by a strong logical or syntactic break at the end of the eighth line. The **Miltonic** sonnet uses the same rhyme pattern but avoids the logical break at the eighth line: it syntactically welds the octave and sestet at an earlier or later place, in counterpoint to the rhyme scheme. The **English** or **Shakespearian** sonnet is divided into one batch of twelve lines followed by a closing couplet. The twelve-line section may be subdivided into three quatrains, and the rhyme scheme for the entire poem is usually *a b a b   c d c d   e f e f   g g.*

The first part of the sonnet traditionally sets up a problem, situation, predicament, or general state of tension or imbalance; it can be called the **complication.** The **resolution** solves the problem, brings out some new realization or development, summarizes the situation, or in some way changes the direction or character of the first part. The point at which the complication pivots into the resolution is the **turn**, or **volta**. Since the content of the sonnet usually parallels the rhyme scheme, the turn appears between the eighth and ninth lines in the Italian sonnet (around the end of the eighth in the Miltonic), and between the twelfth and thirteenth lines in the Shakespearian sonnet.

Because it has been a favorite form in English, the sonnet has been subject to a good deal of experimentation, and not only in mixings of rhyme schemes. A **tailed** or **caudated** sonnet contains additional line fragments after the octave or sestet or both. A **curtal** sonnet contains 10½ lines instead of fourteen but maintains the Italian proportion by having six lines in the first part and 4½ lines in the second part, the final half-line being the **tailpiece**. Also, sonnets have been written in 8s, 6s, and 4s lines.

Rondeau, Rondel: The two terms are used interchangeably, although strictly there is a difference.

The *rondeau*, of fifteen lines, has two main divisions, of which the first may be subdivided into two parts. Each division is followed by a short-line refrain that is a repetition of the first few words of the poem. Not counting this refrain, the entire poem uses only two rhymes: *a a b b a   a a b–R a a b b a–R*.

The *rondel* has fourteen lines and two rhymes. The first line is repeated in its entirety as the seventh and thirteenth line, and the second line is repeated as the eighth and fourteenth line, so that the scheme is *A B b a   a b A B a b b a A B*, where the capitals represent the repeated lines. Both the rondeau and rondel lend themselves to variations.

Epithalamion Stanza: This long, loose stanza of eighteen or nineteen lines has the quality of the ode. There is some variation in the rhyme and meter, but not so much as to distort the character of the stanza. The pattern for the stanzas is usually:

18 lines: $^5 a\,b\,a\,b\,c^3\,c^5\,d\,c\,d\,e^3\,e^5\,f\,g\,g\,f^3\,g^5\,r^6\,R$

19 lines: $^5 a\,b\,a\,b\,c^3\,c^5\,d\,c\,d\,e^3\,e^5\,f\,g\,g\,f\,h^3\,h^5\,r^6\,R,$

where *r* represents the repetition of the same word from stanza to stanza and *R* the repetition of the entire line as a refrain.

Villanelle: This form requires nineteen lines but still permits only two rhymes. It is made of five tercets followed by a final quatrain, where the tercets rhyme *a b a* and the quatrain *a b a a*. Furthermore, the first line must appear in its entirety as lines 6, 12, and 18, while the third line must reappear as lines 9, 15, and 19. The entire scheme is therefore $A'\,b\,A''\quad a\,b\,A'\quad a\,b\,A''\quad a\,b\,A'\quad a\,b\,A''\quad a\,b\,A'\,A''.$

Ballade: not to be confused with the ballad stanza. The ballade is fashioned out of 4s or iambic pentameter lines and contains three stanzas of (usually) eight lines each, rhymed in a fixed order, often the *a b a b b c b C* of the Chaucerian Eight, so that the entire poem may use only three rhymes. The last lines of the stanzas are identical. The three stanzas are followed by an **envoy** of half the number of lines contained in each stanza (therefore usually four), either imitating the stanzaic rhyme scheme or developing a new one, and picking up the refrain. Ballade stanzas are sometimes seven lines long, and sometimes ten.

Sestina: This is a form made of thirty-nine pentameter lines, broken into six stanzas of six lines each, followed by a concluding triplet. The cohesion is provided not by rhyming or repeating lines, but by repetition of the last *word* in each line. The sequence in which these words must occur in any stanza depends on their sequence in the preceding stanza. The word ending the last line of the old stanza must end the *first* line of the new stanza, the one ending the first line of the old now ends the second line of the new, and so forth. If the words ending the lines in a stanza are numbered 1, 2, 3, 4, 5, 6, the following stanza must use them to end its lines in the order 6, 1, 5, 2, 4, 3. Finally, the concluding triplet is seen as composed of six half-lines. The words ending the first three lines of the last normal stanza appear in the same order preceding the cesuras in the three lines of the triplet, while the words ending the last three lines of the last stanza end the lines of the triplet. The repeated-word scheme of the last two stanzas and the concluding triplet may be diagrammed: 1 2 3 4 5 6 − 6 1 5 2 4 3 − 6‖2 1‖4 5‖3.

Ode: *Ode* is a term applied sometimes to a metrical form and sometimes to the general sentiment or tone in a poem without regard to structure. The **Horatian** Ode is characterized more by content than structure: it is mainly lyrical in nature and consists of repeated stanzas. The **Choral** Ode is also characterized by thought and tone, but its form consists of irregular (unpredictable) lines appearing continuously. The **Cowleyan** Ode or **Irregular** Ode, which has been the most popular in English and is also called the **English** Ode, the Pseudo-Pindaric, and the Irregular Pindaric, likewise consists of irregular lines, but the main impression, supported by the typography, is stanzaic rather than continuous. The Cowleyan Ode can be described as consisting of complex stanzas that vary in length, rhyme scheme, line-length, meter, and other facets of general structure. Although the **Pindaric** or **Regular** Ode shares with the others a tendency toward lengthiness, elevation of tone, seriousness of attitude, and general loftiness of effect, it is distinct from them because it follows a strict pattern. It consists of one or ·more groups of three (usually complicated) stanzas each. The first stanza, called the **strophe** or **turn**, may take any form. The second stanza, called the **antistrophe** or **counter-turn**, is metrically identical with the strophe. These are followed by the third stanza, called the **epode** or **stand**, which must be metrically different from the first two. This Regular Pindaric Ode is also called the **Greek Ode**.

APPENDIX 2. CHECKLIST OF RHYMES

By nature of similarity

perfect, full, legitimate, true rhyme: initial consonants of
words differ while stressed vowel and succeeding consonants are the same. *guest/pressed*

slant, half, approximate, near, off, imperfect, oblique rhyme:
stressed vowels are similar but not identical, while
preceding consonants may or may not be identical.
sea/sigh   free/play

identic, identical rhyme: repetition of entire word. Sometimes used for rich rhyme.

rich rhyme: words completely identical in sound but not in
meaning. *flee/flea*

assonant rhyme: vowels are the same but consonants are
different. *cringe/limp*
  assonance: sometimes used for assonant rhyme, but more
  generally an unsystematic recurrence of vowels
  throughout a passage. *spirit ditties of no tone*

consonantal, consonant rhyme: consonants are the same but
vowels are different. *pit/pet/pot*
  consonance: sometimes used for consonant rhyme, but
  more generally an unsystematic recurrence of consonants throughout a passage. *lilies blow*

sight, eye rhyme: similar in spelling but not in pronunciation.
love/move/cove

By relation to stress-pattern

masculine, single rhyme: rhymed element is a concluding
stress. *about/throughout*
       —   —

feminine, double rhyme: rhymed element is a stressed syllable
plus a following slack. *respected/suspected*
$$- \quad x \qquad - \quad x$$

light rhyme: final stress is rhymed with final slack or medial.
infest/conquest   forgive/definitive
$$- \qquad x \qquad - \qquad \hat{-}$$

triple rhyme: rhymed element is a stressed syllable plus two
following slacks. *meticulous/ridiculous*
$$- x \ x \qquad - x \ x$$

multiple rhyme: rhymes involving three or more syllables in
each partner. *references/preferences*
$$- x \ x \ x \qquad - x \ x \ x$$

extended rhyme: rhyming element is extended backward to
involve the slack preceding the rhymed stress.
rhetorical/categorical
$$x - x \ x \qquad x - x \ x$$

By position

end, terminal rhyme: all partners are at the ends of lines.

initial, head rhyme: alliteration.   *furrow   followed   free*

internal rhyme: partners occur anywhere within lines, with
or without partners at the end. Sometimes used for
leonine rhyme.

leonine, medial rhyme: one partner occurs as the last syllable
before the cesura, and the other at the end of the line.
$$a \parallel \ldots a$$
$$b \parallel \ldots b$$

cesural, crossed, interlaced rhyme: in a couplet, the elements
preceding the cesura are partners in their own rhyme.
$$a \parallel \ldots b$$
$$a \parallel \ldots b$$

alternate, interlocking, crossed rhyme: *a b a b.*

intermittent rhyme: *x a x a.*   (Sometimes written *a b c b*).

envelope, inserted rhyme: *a b b a.*

apocopated rhyme: rhymed element is followed by a syllable that does not participate. *believe/relieving*

broken rhyme:
(1)   one of the partners is more than one word.

places/race is

(2)   one partner is the first segment of a word concluded in the following line.   *. . . stopper*

. . . proper

ty.

linked rhyme: one partner completes the rhyme by using the first letter of the following line.   *. . . speed*
(Here, the *d* of *dared* connects   *. . . he*
with *he*, thus making *he-d*   *d(ared to) . . .*
rhyme with *speed*).

analyzed rhyme: in a quatrain, the superimposing of consonantal rhyme in *a b b a* pattern upon assonant rhyme in *a b a b* pattern.

irregular rhyme: the rhyme follows no fixed pattern.

occasional rhyme: only some of the lines are rhymed, and in no fixed pattern.

thorn line: an unrhymed line in a field of mostly rhymed ones.

APPENDIX 3. GLOSSARY

This glossary is intended to be complementary to the index and does not include terms fully described in the text. It is limited to words that have variant definitions, and to words not used here that may be encountered by the student of metrical theory and history.

acatalectic See *catalectic*.

accentual free verse Primary-stress verse, either with a fixed norm or with general limits of variation.

accentual verse Stress-verse. Also, more broadly, any poetry in which metrical status is determined by syllabic accent (as in most English poetry) rather than by syllabic length (as in Greek), syllabic pitch (as in Chinese), etc. See *quantitative verse*.

acephalated, acephalous Truncated.

alteration Decreasing or increasing the number of metrically counted syllables in a line through the process of *compression* (elision or apocopation) or *extension*. That is, counting two syllables of normal pronunciation as metrically one, or the reverse.

ambiguous Not clearly limited to one possible scansion. An ambiguous meter, found most often in stress-verse, is not clearly recognizable, as Common Measure, for example, usually is. It is arrived at only as the metrist determines what kind of pattern the lines will best qualify for; it is a *qualified meter*. An *indeterminate* line is similarly ambiguous, and so also a *doubtful* syllable, called *anceps*, which by virtue of its being *medial* or *common* may be scanned either as stress or slack. If the metrist leaves such ambiguities *undecided* his scansion of the line remains *unresolved* or *optional*, and the metrical norm itself may be *undetermined*. These are not strict terms. See *resolution*.

ametric Non-metric, not measurable under a given system.

anceps See *ambiguous*.

arsis See *thesis*.

atonic Without accent or stress. Nonaccentual in the sense of not using contrastive stress as a basis for scansion, as in Greek (quantitative) or French (syllabic) verse.

augmentation Of stanza: enlarging a stanza by adding lines or fragments. Of sounds: using two sounds adjacently and then repeating them, but this time with one or more sounds intervening. The reverse of this process (as in *fie̲lds where fl̲ies*) is called *diminution*.

ballad meter, ballad stanza Folk Meter, but often applied to Common Measure specifically, especially when in duple-triple rhythm. When the 4−3−4−3 stress-pattern occurs in perfect duple rhythm it is also called the *hymnal stanza*. See *Common Measure*.

bar A measured section of rhythm; a foot; a subdivision of a line, containing a stress plus all rhythmical features up to the next stress. Also, a vertical mark to symbolize foot boundaries.

base, metrical base Norm. As described by Professor Barkas (see *Suggested Readings*): "The phonetic rhythm has been so highly generalized and idealized in the patterns, that the same pattern must recur frequently and that patterns which differ must be identical in some of their parts. These similarities and identities suggest the idea of a single typical pattern, perfectly regular in structure, as the norm to which all the rhythmical patterns found in verse of the same kind can be referred. Such norms are called Metrical Bases." See *compound base*.

base structure   The main structure of a form (especially a stanza) after the superstructure (refrains, repetitions, etc.) is removed.

bastard foot   Having an extra slack to be pronounced quickly and lightly.   The word *delicate* exemplifies a bastard trochee.

blank stress   Ictus.

brachycatalectic   A line deficient by an entire foot.   The concept is useful only where double feet are involved, as in dipodic verse.   Common Measure, where the arsis of the final dipod is replaced by a pause, can be referred to as brachycatalectic, although the information would be redundant.

breathing   A pause, but not fixed at one place or given metrical value.

burden, burthen   Refrain.   A *burden line* is a chorus-like coda ending on the same words that end the preceding staple line.

cantillation   Chanting, intoning, reciting musically.

catalectic   Deficiency by a slack syllable.   *Acatalectic* means not deficient and is useful only where catalexis is expected or frequent.

catch   Anacrusis.

centroid   See *stress-center*.

cesura, caesura   The "cutting" of the line by a sense-pause (as distinct from a metrical pause).   Sometimes used for what we call *apocopation*.   Also possibly for what we call *linking*, since in classical prosody cesura is the opposite of *dieresis*.

checked   A foot or line lacking one or more final slack syllables.

chorus   Refrain.

cinquepace   Iambic pentameter.

clipped line   Generally, a truncated line; specifically, the seven-syllable, four-stress line, appearing either as a variant to iambic tetrameter or octosyllabics, or as a norm in itself, when it is also called the *upcast line.*

coalition   The fusing of two words through the loss (elision) of a syllable.

coda, cauda   "Tail":   a group concluding a passage and shorter than the staplę lines.

Common Measure, Common Meter   The seven-stress Folk Meter that breaks into hemistichs in the 4—3p—4—3p pattern. The term is often limited, however, to the *hymnal stanza,* which has a perfect count of 8—6—8—6 syllables. See *ballad meter.*

common rhythm   Sometimes: regular duple rhythm, by analogy to the "common" rhythm of the hymns. But also applied to *running rhythm* (foot-verse capable of being counterpointed), called also *standard rhythm,* as opposed to *sprung rhythm.*

common section   Amphibious section.

common syllable   A medial syllable. See *ambiguous.*

complement   A section that unites with another section (its own complement) to complete a metrically full line, usually iambic pentameter.

compound base   The structural appearance of a poem where the basic pattern can be regarded in more than one dimension. For example, the hymnal stanza has a syllabic base, a stress base, and a syllable-stress (foot) base.

concatenatio   The device of repeating the final words of a stanza as the opening words of the following stanza, possibly with slight changes. Cf. *verse-capping.*

configurational Any metrical system in which some syllables are more important than others, creating contrasts upon which the system is based.

contraction Compression, elision.

coordination Agreement of meter and prose rhythm in the words of a poem. Cf. *syncopation.*

crasis Elision.

crest See *stress-center.*

cumulative rhythm The large, general cadences made of groups of lines.

cynghanedd A complicated and strict arrangement of stress-pattern, alliteration, and rhyme. Apparently workable only in Welsh poetry, but sometimes approximated in English.

delivery instance The phonetic pattern rendered in the actual utterance (*performance*) of a line of poetry, as opposed to the *verse instance* of the line seen as a meter-rhythm compromise and rendered in the scansion, and the *verse design*, the abstract metrical norm.

demotion Regarding a secondary stress as metrically slack.

density The proportion of rhythmical to metrical stresses. The more demotions, the greater the density.

depressed Unstressed, unimportant syllable. At one time confused with a quantitatively short syllable.

determined A syllable settled by the metrist as counting either as stress or slack, or a line whose scansion has been decided upon. Cf. *ambiguous.*

differential The relative degree of difference between the general stress-level and slack-level in a cadence, line, stanza, or poem.

dilation Extension.

diminution See *augmentation.*

displacement of stress   Arrangement of words in a poem so that the stress tends to be pronounced isochronously early or late, causing *syncopation*.   Also sometimes used for *stress-shift*.

distich   Two lines connected in some way, not necessarily through rhyme or meter (which would create a couplet).

distortion   The stylization of normal prose rhythm under the influence of a metrical pattern, causing some words to be pronounced with a certain artificiality.

distributed stress   See *hovering accent*.

disyllabist   One who allows the compression of two syllables into one in scansion.

double audition   The perception of a discrepancy between metrical pattern and actual pronunciation.

duple-duple rhythm   The | — x ˆ x | cadence, seen as both the paeonic | — x x x | and the dipodic | ⁔ x ⁔ x | counterpointing each other, and sometimes said to be *syncopated*.

elegiac couplet, distich   One pentameter followed by one hexameter.   The *elegiac stanza*, or *quatrain*, is the pentameter *abab* quatrain.

end-stopped   Estopped.

epode   The third part of the stanza-cluster in the Pindaric Ode.   Also: a form where longer and shorter lines alternate, as in Poulter's Measure, broken Common Measure, or elegiac couplets.

equivalence   The principle under which syllables of certain total metrical value are accepted as legitimate substitutes for others (as a trochaic cadence may be substituted for a dactylic one).

expansion   Extension.   Also: the lengthening of lines by allowing them extra stresses.

feminine meter   Linkage.

feminine rhyme, feminine ending   Generally, ending on a slack. Specifically: ending the line with a final *e* that is now no longer pronounced.

field   Metrical context; overall structural situation.

Fifteenth-century Heroic   A line akin to the iambic pentameter, conceived as divided into two sections each allowing two or three stresses, so that the full-line has from four to six stresses, commonly five.

filling-in   Pronouncing syllables formerly lost through elision.

free-ended   Lines free to be estopped or enjambed, and usually enjambed. Also: the opposite of *rove-over*.

gap, gappage, gaping   Hiatus.

gemell, geminell lines   Heroic couplets.

ground rhythm   The rhythm heard when both primary and secondary stresses (called *ground stresses*) are taken as *markers*, rendering the meter at the *ground level*. For example, ground rhythm would render a falling dipod ($\acute{-}$ x $\acute{-}$ x) where the *primary rhythm*, hearkening after the *primary* stresses *only*, would render the same passage as a paeonic ($-$ x x x).

half stress   Medial stress.

hanger   An *outride*.

headless   Truncated.

head rhyme   Alliteration.

head-stave   The sound alliterated by the *rhyme-giver*.

hiatus   The situation where a word ending in a vowel is followed by one beginning with a vowel (*the evening*) and the *opening* or *gap* is not closed through compression. (The compressed form would be pronounced *th'evening*).

hold   Sustaining the pronunciation of a syllable in order to preserve isochronism; a type of metrical *pause*.

hovering accent, hovering stress, distributed stress The metrical assignment of one stress to *two* adjacent syllables; the scansion of two adjacent secondary stresses to count as a single metrical *stress-center*; the rendering of an *unresolved* scansion, leaving the assignment of a stress to one of two adjacent syllables *optional.*

hymnal stanza See *ballad meter; Common Measure.*

ictus Stress awarded in scansion on the basis of metrical need rather than on the natural importance or prominence of the syllable; promotion. Also called *metrical stress, blank stress.*

identic A word repeated in its entirety to fulfill a structural requirement, such as the *identic rhyme* of the sestina.

indeterminate norm See *ambiguous.*

intensity The loudness with which a syllable is pronounced.

interplay Counterpoint; tension between rhythm and meter.

isoaccentual System of meter in which syllables are given configurational prominence according to accent or stress.

isochronous, isochronic, isochronism System of meter in which the main organizing feature is the equality of time intervals between stresses.

isosyllabic System of meter in which the main organizing feature is the equality in the total number of syllables (nonconfigurational) from line to line.

isosyntactic System of meter in which the main organizing feature is the repetition of phrases or syntactic constructions.

isotonic System of meter in which syllables are given configurational prominence according to pitch.

lengthened line Any line longer than the staple given in its context. More particularly, the Anglo-Saxon alliterative line containing three rather than two primary stresses in one or both hemistichs, creating a full-line of five or six stresses (cf. *Fifteenth-century Heroic*). Sometimes: an alexandrine among pentameters.

lengthening   Extension.

limerick   A comic poem consisting of one couplet of accentual Poulter's Measure with fixed (internal) rhyme: $^3aa^2bb^3a$.

line-duel   Stichomythia.

logaoedic   Duple-triple rhythms approximating prose rhythm. Mixed meters generally.

long alexandrine   Septenary.

long line   Long Measure.   Also: the full-line of the Anglo-Saxon Alliterative Verse.

marker, point, support   Any element significant in the organization of metrical structure, distinct from similar but insignificant elements; as, for example, a syllable given *configurational* prominence.   Thus stress-verse carries markers in its stressed syllables, while pure syllabic verse need have none because it depends on mere count of total number of syllables.

masculine meter   Dieresis.

melos   That aspect of poetry analogous to music.

metrical pause, metrical silence   See *pause*.

metrical stress   Ictus.

modal shift   Changing from one more or less established mode in a poem to another, as in creating triple rhythms among a *field* of duples.

modification   Producing variety in a metrical line by modifying the prose stresses through promotion or demotion.

modulation   Shifting from one kind of apparent metrical structure to another, such as in modal shift.   Also: *distortion* or stylization of pronunciation in order to preserve the meter through modification and alteration; rhythm when heard in contrast to meter; counterpoint; differential.

monopod   Single (standard) foot, as opposed to the ionic or dipodic double-feet.

monostich   One full-line. Cf. *hemistich; distich.*

mora   The time occupied by a quantitatively short syllable.

mounted rhythm   The rhythm created by substitutions or by counterpoint generally; the rhythmic compromise between meter and prose rhythm.

musical pause   See *pause.*

numbers   Meter; particularly isosyllabic meter, dependent on the number of syllables per line.

octet   Octave (of sonnet).

octosyllabics   A four-stress line, usually in duple rhythm, containing 7 to 9 syllables but usually 8.

optional norm   See *ambiguous.*

outride   One, two, or three slacks added to a foot and regarded as hypermetrical.

particular meter   An augmented Folk Meter stanza consisting of six hemistichs rather than the basic four. Used almost exclusively with reference to hymns, the term denotes the number of syllables rather than the number of stresses per hemistich. *Common Particular Meter* is a stanza of 8–8–6–8–8–6 syllables (making a stress-pattern of 4–4–3–4–4–3); *Long Particular Meter* is a stanza of 8–8–8–8–8–8 syllables (making all four-stress lines); and *Short Particular Meter* is a stanza of 6–6–8–6–6–8 syllables (making a 3–3–4–3–3–4 stress-pattern).

partner   A verbal unit participating in rhyme.

pause, silence   Temporary suspension of reading, classified into two main types: (1) *logical, syntactic, cesural, sense, suspensory pause* is an indefinite interruption in accordance with logic, meaning, and prose rhythm; (2) *metrical, musical, compensatory pause, rest, hold* is an interruption in accordance with metrical requirements and is given an isochronously fixed metrical value, functional in the Folk Meters. The two may be distinguished simply as *cesura* and *pause*.

pause-foot   A foot made up entirely of silence.

pentapody   A five-foot line.

performance   See *delivery instance.*

point   See *marker.*

prepositional stress   Ictus given to a preposition.

primary rhythm   See *ground rhythm.*

progression   The general developing pattern (e.g., circular, sequential) in a batch of instances of some feature (e.g., syllable-count, stress-count, number of cadences per strophe), seen as retrospective form.

promotion   Regarding a tertiary stress as metrically stressed.

prosody   The study of versification and other organizations of language.

qualified meter   See *ambiguous.*

quantitative verse   Verse based on the length of syllables, in the strict form of which two *short* syllables are *equivalent* to one *long.* Classical verse. Never completely achieved in English, which depends on *qualitative* stress rather than quantitative length.

reading time unit   Cadence.   At times regarded as a sub-division of the cadence in CFV.   CFV, however, is not rigid

enough to make many profitable distinctions between
unit, cadence, and strophe.

recovery   Return to the norm after one or more inversions,
usually signaled by a modal shift in the rhythm.

representative verse   A line whose scansion is metrically
perfect, rendering the matrix; a line that reproduces the
norm without variations.

resolution   In classical prosody, the substitution of two
quantitatively short syllables for one long. In accentual
verse, the replacement of one slack by two or the substitution of a trisyllabic foot for a disyllabic one, especially
an anapest for an iamb. Also: the completion of an
expected pattern in a stanza (cf. *suspended resolution*); the
concluding (problem-solving) part of a sonnet. Also: the
deciding of a metrical ambiguity.

resolved foot   One containing more than two syllables. Also:
a trisyllabic foot counting as disyllabic by virtue of elision.

resolved meter   Decided-upon. Cf. *ambiguous.* Also: meter
using elisions.

rest   See *pause.*

reversed foot   Inversion.

rhyme-giver   The first stressed syllable in the second hemistich of alliterative verse, in cases where it can be depended
upon to carry the alliteration.

riding rhyme, riding rhythm   Heroic couplets; decasyllabic
couplets; iambic pentameter.

rocking rhythm, rocking foot   Cadence where a stress falls
between two slacks; amphibrachic.

rove-over lines   Where the scanning is continued uninter-
rupted to the end of the stanza, so that an extra slack at
the end of a line would mean one fewer slack beginning the

next line. The opposite of *free-ended* lines, where each line is scanned by itself. Also called *synaphea.*

roving accent   Stress-verse, duple-triple, tumbling verse; non-foot-verse; meter that prescribes the number but not the position of stresses in the line.

running rhythm   See *common rhythm.*

Schwellvers   Alliterative line lengthened to three primary stresses in each hemistich.

section   One of the two portions of the iambic pentameter line created by the cesura; a subdivision of any line having four or more stresses; any verse division larger than a foot.

septet, sextet, sextain   Sestet.

shaped poetry   Poetry appearing typographically in representational forms (such as wings) or abstract designs (such as triangles).

shift   See *modal shift; stress-shift.*

shortening   Elision.

Short Meter   Sometimes used to denote what is called Half Meter in this book, but ordinarily denotes Poulter's Measure with a regularized stress-count of 6–6–8–6 syllables, as found in many hymns.

Sievers   Eduard Sievers classified the rhythmic patterns of the Anglo-Saxon alliterative hemistichs, counting both stresses and slacks. For example, "Sievers Type C" is | x – – x |.

silence   See *pause.*

single-molded   End-stopped. Also: free-ended (as opposed to rove-over).

single rhythm   Made of adjacent stresses, used only as a momentary rhythmic shift in duple or duple-triple rhythm. Sometimes used of duple rhythm itself.

skeltonic verse Rhymed short lines (usually two-stress) with rough, jagged rhythm.

slack A syllable not counting as a metrical stress. Also: the unstressed portion of a foot, containing zero, one, two, or sometimes more syllables.

standard rhythm See *common rhythm*.

staple, stock The standard norm of which most of the lines in a metrical context are made.

stichomythia In dramatic or pseudo-dramatic poetry, a *line-duel* in which each speaker uses exactly one line at a time, and the two speakers exchange lines alternately.

stress Metrical emphasis, prominence, or importance of a syllable, as opposed to the *accent* given a syllable in prose utterance.

stress-center The *crest* of a rhythmical *wave* in a line where the cadence builds to a metrically weighted phrase; generally, configurational prominence given to a batch of syllables rather than to a single one. Also: hovering stress. Also: a *centroid*, the imaginary point at which all the configurationally prominent features are thought to be concentrated, allowing the metrist to determine the norm without resolving the scansion entirely. Also: the place in the line where stresses are jammed.

stress failure Promotion in a foot that has no naturally strong stresses.

stress-shift Inversion.

strong-stress Stress-verse.

supernumerary Extrametrical, hypermetric, redundant.

support See *marker*.

suppression Demotion.

suspended resolution Delaying the expected conclusion of a stanza.

suspensory pause   See *pause.*

syllabism   Counting the total number of syllables in a line.

synaphea   See *rove-over.*

syncopation   (1) Displacement of stress. (2) Duple-duple rhythm. (3) Counterpoint. Cf. *coordination.*

syzygy   Combining two feet, sometimes two different kinds of feet, into a single metrical unit.

thesis   The primary stress in a dipod; the place occupied by the primary stress of a dipod; a metrically stressed syllable. *Arsis* refers to the secondary stress in a dipod, or the place occupied by it, or any slack, or any part of a foot other than the stress. Many metrists use the two terms the other way around.

tirade   A group of lines, such as a verse paragraph or non-stanzaic strophe.

tumbling   Duple-triple stress-verse.

tumbling ending   Having two extra slacks at the end.

undetermined, unresolved syllable   See *ambiguous.*

unstressed syllable   Slack.

upcast line   See *clipped line.*

vanishing   Elision.

variation   Exception to metrical rule. *Secondary* variations are those that do not become standard amendments to metrical law; *permissive variations* are those agreed upon tacitly by poets as permitted; *primary variations* are those that become traditional.

verse   (1) Poetry. (2) One line of metrical poetry. (3) Stanza.

verse-capping   The device of repeating the last letter in a line as the first letter in the following line written in the same meter. Cf. *concatenatio.*

verse design, verse instance See *delivery instance*.

versification The rules governing the metrical treatment of poetry.

versi sciolti Unrhymed poetry.

vers libre Free verse; poetry not containing predictable abstract forms. In French, poetry not using fixed syllable-counts.

visual syllabics Syllabic verse whose structure is not heard but seen on the page.

wave See *stress-center*.

weak ending Light ending. Also: extrametric, redundant.

weak measure Foot in which the stress is in *ictus*.

wheel stanza Stanza in which the frons and cauda are connected by a regular staple rather than by a bob.

wrenched accent Stress-shift; inversion. Also: distortion of the normal stress-pattern of a word.

APPENDIX 4. SUGGESTED READINGS

Classifications and Illustrations of Metrical Forms

Alden, Raymond MacDonald. *English Verse. Specimens Illustrating Its Principles and History.* New York, 1903.
Kaluza, Max. *A Short History of English Versification.* London and New York, 1911.
Schipper, Jakob. *A History of English Versification.* Oxford, 1910.

Metrical Theory

Barkas, Pallister. *A Critique of Modern English Prosody (1880–1930).* Halle (Saale), 1934.
Baum, Paull Franklin. *The Principles of English Versification.* Cambridge, Mass., 1923.
Lanier, Sidney. *The Science of English Verse.* Baltimore, 1945.
Mayor, Joseph B. *Chapters on English Metre.* Cambridge, England, 1901.
Nabokov, Vladimir. *Notes on Prosody.* Bollingen, 1965.
Stewart, George R. "The Meter of the Popular Ballad." *PMLA*, XL (1925), 933–962.
Young, Sir George. *An English Prosody on Inductive Lines.* London, 1928.

The Esthetics of Meter

Coleridge, Samuel Taylor. *Biographia Literaria*, 1817. Chapter XVIII.
Eliot, T.S. "The Music of Poetry," *On Poetry and Poets.* London, 1957; New York, 1961.
Frye, Northrop. *Anatomy of Criticism.* Princeton, 1957.
Gross, Harvey. *Sound and Form in Modern Poetry.* Ann Arbor, 1964.

Gummere, Francis B. "Rhythm as the Essential Fact of Poetry," *The Beginnings of Poetry*. New York, 1908.

Malof, Joseph. "Meter as Organic Form." *Modern Language Quarterly*, XXVII (March 1966), 3–17.

Ransom, John Crowe. *The New Criticism.* Norfolk, 1941.

Winters, Yvor. *Primitivism and Decadence.* New York, 1937.

Wordsworth, William. Preface to *Lyrical Ballads,* 1800.

History

Allen, Gay Wilson. *American Prosody.* New York, 1935.

Culler, A. Dwight. "Edward Bysshe and the Poet's Handbook." *PMLA*, LXIII (1948), 858–885.

Gummere, Francis B. "The Translation of Beowulf, and the Relations of Ancient and Modern English Verse." *American Journal of Philology,* VII (1886), 46–78.

Ing, Catherine. *Elizabethan Lyrics.* London, 1951.

Leonard, William Ellery. "*Beowulf* and the Nibelungen Couplet." *University of Wisconsin Studies in Language and Literature*, No. 2 (Sept., 1918), pp. 99–152.

Lewis, Charlton M. *The Foreign Sources of Modern English Versification.* Yale Studies in English, 1898.

Lewis, C. S. "The Fifteenth-century Heroic Line," *Essays and Studies,* XXIV (1938). Oxford, 1939, pp. 28–41.

Malof, Joseph. "The Native Rhythm of English Meters." *Texas Studies in Literature and Language*, V (1964), 580–594.

Omond, T. S. *English Metrists.* Oxford, 1921.

Saintsbury, George. *Historical Manual of English Prosody.* London, 1914.

Thompson, John. *The Founding of English Metre.* New York, 1961.

Wallerstein, Ruth. "The Development of the Rhetoric and Metre of the Heroic Couplet, Especially in 1625–1645." *PMLA*, L (1935), 166–209.

Wells, Henry W. *New Poets from Old.* New York, 1940.

Westlake, John S. "The Old English Sung, or Ballad, Metre." Appendix to Chapter VII of *The Cambridge History of English Literature.* New York and Cambridge, England, 1933, pp. 461–468.

Studies of Individual Poets: A Sampling

Adler, Jacob H. "Pope and the Rules of Prosody." *PMLA*, LXXVI (1961), 218–226.

Baum, P.F. *Chaucer's Verse*. Durham, 1961.

Bradley, Sculley. "The Fundamental Metrical Principle in Whitman's Poetry." *American Literature*, X (1939), 437–459.

Bridges, Robert. *Milton's Prosody*. Oxford, 1921.

Hopkins, Gerard Manley. "Author's Preface," *Poems*. London, 1918.

McNaughton, William. "Ezra Pound's Meters and Rhythms." *PMLA*, LXXVIII (1963), 136–146.

Moloney, Michael F. "Donne's Metrical Practice." *PMLA*, LXV (1950), 232–239.

Pope, John C. *The Rhythm of Beowulf*. New Haven, 1942.

Pyre, F. F. A. *The Formation of Tennyson's Style*. Madison, 1921.

Southworth, James G. *Verses of Cadence. An Introduction to the Prosody of Chaucer and his Followers*. Oxford, 1954.

Sprott, S. Ernest. *Milton's Art of Prosody*. Oxford, 1953.

Recent Discussions

Allen, Charles. "Cadenced Free Verse." *College English*, IX (1948), 195–199.

Chatman, Seymour, John Crowe Ransom, Arnold Stein, and Harold Whitehall. "English Verse and What It Sounds Like." *Kenyon Review*, XVIII (1956), 411–477.

Chatman, Seymour. *A Theory of Meter*. The Hague, 1965.

Epstein, Edmund L. and Terence Hawkes. *Linguistics and English Prosody*. Buffalo, 1959.

Fussell, Paul, Jr. *Poetic Meter and Poetic Form*. New York, 1965.

Halpern, Martin. "On the Two Chief Metrical Modes in English." *PMLA*, LXXVII (1962), 177–186.

Lewis, C. S. "Metre." *Review of English Literature* (Leeds), I (1960), 45–50.

Malof, Joseph. "The Artifice of Scansion." *English Journal,* LIV (December 1965), 857–860, 871.

Sebeok, Thomas A., ed. *Style in Language.* New York, 1960.

Whitehall, Harold. "From Linguistics to Poetry," in Northrop Frye, ed., *Sound and Poetry,* New York, 1957, pp. 134–145.

Whitmore, Charles E. "A Proposed Compromise in Metrics." *PMLA,* XLI (1926), 1024–43.

Wimsatt, W. K. and Monroe C. Beardsley. "The Concept of Meter: An Exercise in Abstraction." *PMLA,* LXXIV (1959), 585–598.

General

Deutsch, Babette. *Poetry Handbook. A Dictionary of Terms.* New York, 1957.

Gross, Harvey, ed. *The Structure of Verse: Modern Essays on Prosody.* Fawcett Books, 1966.

Hemphill, George, ed. *Discussions of Poetry: Rhythm and Sound.* Boston, 1961.

Hungerford, Edward B. *Recovering the Rhythms of Poetry: The Elements of Versification.* Chicago, 1964.

Murphy, Francis. *Discussions of Poetry: Form and Structure.* Boston, 1964.

Shapiro, Karl. *A Bibliography of Modern Prosody.* Baltimore, 1948.

Shapiro, Karl, and Robert Beum. *A Prosody Handbook.* New York, 1965.

Smith, Barbara Herrnstein. *Poetic Closure: A Study of How Poems End.* Chicago, 1968.

Turco, Lewis. *The Book of Forms: A Handbook of Poetics.* New York, 1968.

APPENDIX 5. KEY TO QUOTED POEMS

page

61 "What sense . . ." Shakespeare: *Othello*.
61 "No, faith . . ." Shakespeare: *Othello*.
62 "Edward's . . ." Shakespeare: *Richard the Second*.
62 "Stiffly . . ." Jonson: Epilogue to *Cynthia's Revels*.
62 "Anguish . . ." Milton: *Paradise Lost*, I.
62 "Of Rainbows . . ." Milton: *Paradise Lost*, VII.
62 "Created . . ." Milton: *Paradise Lost*, I.
62 "So he . . ." Milton: *Paradise Lost*, II.
63 "For me . . ." Pope: *Essay on Man*.
63 "Became . . ." Shakespeare: *Henry the Fourth*, Part II.
63 "All the sad . . ." Keats: *Hyperion*, II.
63 "And yet . . ." Shakespeare: *Hamlet*.
63 "But Brutus . . ." Shakespeare: *Julius Caesar*.
63 "To woo . . ." Shakespeare: *The Merchant of Venice*.
64 "And think . . ." Shakespeare: *Henry the Fourth*, Part I.
64 "Ne may . . ." Spenser: *Faerie Queene*, III.
64 "That sayd . . ." Spenser: *Faerie Queene*, III.
65 "Your daughter . . ." Shakespeare: *As You Like It*.
65 "When to . . ." Shakespeare: Sonnet 30.
67 "The world . . ." G. M. Hopkins: "God's Grandeur."
68 "Before . . ." Milton: *Paradise Lost*, VI.
68 "To be . . ." Shakespeare: *Hamlet*.
69 "Nor streit'ning . . ." Milton: *Paradise Lost*, VI.
69 "She sang . . ." Wallace Stevens: "The Idea of Order at Key West."
70 "Yet it . . ." Marvell: "The Garden."
70 "And the wheel's . . ." Masefield: "Sea-Fever."
70 "I sought . . ." Yeats: "The Circus Animals' Desertion."
71 "On the rich . . ." Pope: *The Rape of the Lock*.
72 "Still through . . ." E. A. Robinson: "Octaves."
73 "A pig . . ." John Crowe Ransom: "Dead Boy."
73 "It looked . . ." Robert Frost: "Once By the Pacific."
74 "If thou . . ." Shakespeare: *Julius Caesar*.
74 "When I . . ." Shakespeare: *Henry the Fourth*, Part I.
74 "But short . . ." Dryden: "The Medal."
75 "Held up . . ." T. S. Eliot: *The Waste Land*.

page

75 "Send out . . ." Shakespeare: *Macbeth.*
75 "Almighty . . ." Dryden: "The Medal."
76 "From me . . ." Shakespeare: *Hamlet.*
76 "That huge . . ." Dryden: *Marriage à la Mode.*
77 "What, all . . ." Shakespeare: *Macbeth.*
77 "The weariest . . ." Shakespeare: *Measure for Measure.*
79 "Getting . . ." Wordsworth: "The World is Too Much With Us."
79 "When to . . ." Shakespeare: Sonnet 30.
82 "When men . . ." Robert Bridges: "London Snow."
82 "I have heard . . ." Yeats: "Lapis Lazuli."
83 "Gib . . ." Skelton: "Philip Sparrow."
83 "Whan that . . ." Chaucer: General Prologue to *The Canterbury Tales.*
84 "For had . . ." Spenser: "September."
84 "Captain . . ." John Crowe Ransom: "Captain Carpenter."
84 "What art . . ." Shakespeare: *Hamlet.*
85 "I can . . ." Longfellow: "My Lost Youth."
85 "I have . . ." G. M. Hopkins: "Heaven-Haven."
85 "Beautifully . . ." John Crowe Ransom: "Janet Waking."
86 "Get up . . ." Herrick: "Corinna's Going A-Maying."
86 "After . . ." T. S. Eliot: *The Waste Land.*
87 "Stop . . ." W. H. Auden: "Stop All the Clocks."
90 "Wæs sē . . ." *Beowulf.*
90 "Bitter breast-cares . . ." Ezra Pound, transl.: "The Seafarer."
92 "An axe . . ." Richard Wilbur: "Junk."
93 "Our king . . ." "The Bonny Lass of Anglesey" (ballad).
94 "Then they . . ." "Dick O the Cow" (ballad).
95 "Nay, were . . ." "Bewick and Graham" (ballad).
95 "Come, sound . . ." "The Young Earl of Essex's Victory Over the Emperor of Germany" (ballad).
95 "The king . . ." "The Outlaw Murray" (ballad).
96 "The modest . . ." Blake: "The Lilly."
96 "How the . . ." Blake: "London."
96 "And on . . ." Byron: "She Walks in Beauty."
97 "Comrades, leave . . ." Tennyson: "Locksley Hall."

page

97 "Safe in . . ." Emily Dickinson: "Safe in their alabaster chambers."

97 "He will . . ." Emily Dickinson: "I shall know why, when time is over."

97 "But one . . ." Wilde: "Impression du Matin."

97 "What need . . ." Yeats: "September 1913."

98 "Donne, I suppose . . ." T. S. Eliot: "Whispers of Immortality."

98 "The host . . ." T. S. Eliot: "Sweeney Among the Nightingales."

98 "septembering . . ." E. E. Cummings: "My Father Moved Through Dooms of Love."

98 "stars rain . . ." E. E. Cummings: "Anyone Lived in a Pretty How Town."

98 "'O where . . .'" W. H. Auden: "O Where Are You Going?"

99 "Edgar Degas . . ." Richard Wilbur: "Museum Piece."

99 "Infant . . ." Wallace Stevens: "The Red Fern."

101 "The king . . ." "Sir Patrick Spens" (ballad).

103 "Our king . . ." "Lord Derwentwater" (ballad).

104 "Her pretty . . ." Herrick: "Upon Mistress Susanna Southwell Her Feet."

104 "Sigh no more . . ." Shakespeare: *Much Ado About Nothing.*

104 "For Mercy . . ." Blake: "The Divine Image."

105 "Gaily bedight . . ." Poe: "Eldorado."

105 "I must . . ." Masefield: "Sea-fever."

105 "The yellow . . ." T. S. Eliot: "The Love Song of J. Alfred Prufrock."

105 "When man . . ." E. E. Cummings: "When God Decided to Invent."

105 "Straddling . . ." Yeats: "News for the Delphic Oracle."

108 "The first . . ." "Hugh Spencer's Feats in France" (ballad).

108 "Ye Highlands . . ." "The Bonny Earl of Murray" (ballad).

page

116 "The garden . . ." Wallace Stevens: "The Pleasures of Merely Circulating."
117 "And what . . ." "Edward" (ballad).
118 "All delicate . . ." Swinburne: "Hymn to Proserpine."
118 "Through twenty . . ." Chapman: *The Iliad*, XVIII.
119 "O let . . ." Redford: *Marriage of Wit and Science.*
119 "The nurse . . ." Brooke: *Romeus and Juliet.*
120 "Each beast . . ." Surrey: "Of a Lady that Refused to Dance with Him."
120 "And have . . ." Howard Chandler Robbins: "And Have the Bright Immensities."
121 " 'Twas brillig . . ." Lewis Carroll: "Jabberwocky."
121 "But now . . ." John Crowe Ransom: "Bells for John Whiteside's Daughter."
121 "I set . . ." Keats: "La Belle Dame Sans Merci."
121 "I've known . . ." Emily Dickinson: "The Soul Selects Her Own Society."
122 "But, Mousie . . ." Burns: "To a Mouse."
122 "His sheeld . . ." Chaucer: "Sir Thopas."
123 "With throats . . ." Coleridge: *The Rime of the Ancient Mariner.*
123 "She fears . . ." E. A. Robinson: "Eros Turannos."
123 "When I . . ." Christina Rossetti: "Song."
124 "Fear no more . . ." Shakespeare: *Cymbeline.*
124 "Under . . ." Shakespeare: *As You Like It.*
124 "Full fathom . . ." Shakespeare: *The Tempest.*
125 "Have you . . ." Jonson: "Her Triumph."
125 "A route . . ." Emily Dickinson: "A Route of Evanescence."
132 "Beat . . ." Vachel Lindsay: "The Congo."
135 "If you're . . ." Kipling: "Philadelphia."
136 "Under yonder . . ." Meredith: "Love in the Valley."
137 "The yellow . . ." T. S. Eliot: "The Love Song of J. Alfred Prufrock."
139 "Let us . . ." Marvell: "To His Coy Mistress."

page

140 "While I . . ." A. M. Toplady: "A Prayer, Living and Dying."

140 "Confirm . . ." Winfred Douglas: "Awake, My Heart."

140 "It has . . ." Donald Hall: "Je Suis Une Table."

141 "I wake . . ." G. M. Hopkins: "I Wake and Feel the Fell of Dark, Not Day."

141 "One drop . . ." Robert Frost: "For Once, Then, Something."

142 "When Summer . . ." Surrey: *Poems of Love and Chivalry*, V.

143 "except . . ." E. E. Cummings: "except in your."

143 "Although . . ." Marianne Moore: "He 'Digesteth Harde Yron.'"

145 "Lord . . ." George Herbert: "Easter Wings."

148 "It is night . . ." James Macpherson: "The Songs of Selma."

148 "Go thy way . . ." *Ecclesiastes*, 9.

149 "By degrees . . ." Blake: *The Marriage of Heaven and Hell.*

149 "And indeed . . ." T. S. Eliot: "The Love Song of J. Alfred Prufrock."

150 "She put . . ." *Judges*, 5.

150 "None . . ." Whitman: "To You."

150 "Each . . ." Whitman: "Salut Au Monde!"

151 "The inner . . ." T. S. Eliot: "Burnt Norton."

152 "Internal . . ." T. S. Eliot: "Burnt Norton."

152 "The song . . ." Whitman: "A Song of the Rolling Earth."

153 "To communicate . . ." T. S. Eliot: "The Dry Salvages."

154 "The magic . . ." Shelley: *Queen Mab*, II.

156 "Underneath . . ." Amy Lowell: "Patterns."

160 "I don't . . ." Sandburg: "Ossawatomie."

161 "Though . . ." Skelton: "Colyn Cloute."

161 "To A Snail," by Marianne Moore.

163 "If we . . ." T. S. Eliot: *The Cocktail Party.*

167 "When I . . ." Milton: "Sonnet on His Blindness."

167 "Of Mans . . ." Milton: *Paradise Lost*, I.

APPENDIX 6. SHORT SUMMARY OF FORMS

A. Folk Lines

alliterative verse: $\underline{(k)}$ $\underline{(k)}$ ‖ $\underline{k}$ — (2–2)

Long Measure: — — — — ‖ — — — — or $\begin{cases} - - - - \, \| \\ \\ - - - - \end{cases}$ (4–4)

Common Measure: — — — — ‖ — — — (p) or $\begin{cases} - - - - \, \| \\ \\ - - - \, (p) \end{cases}$ (4–3)

Half Measure: — — — (p)‖ — — — (p) or $\begin{cases} - - - \, (p) \| \\ \\ - - - \, (p) \end{cases}$ (3–3)

Poulter's Measure: — — — (p)‖ — — — (p)
 — — — — ‖ — — — (p)

or $\begin{cases} - - - \, (p) \| \\ - - - \, (p) \\ - - - - \, \| \\ - - - \, (p) \end{cases}$ (3–3–4–3)

or $\begin{cases} - - - \, (p) \| \\ - - - \, (p) \\ - - \\ - \, - \| \\ - - - \, (p) \end{cases}$

B. Rhythms and Cadences

duple rhythm: . . . x — x — x — x . . . .

triple rhythm: . . . x x — x x — x x — x x . . . .

duple-triple rhythm: . . . x — — x — x x — x — x x — x x — . . . .

duple-duple rhythm: ... $- x \doteq x - x \doteq x - x \doteq x$ ....

pyrrhic cadence: | x x |

spondaic cadence: | − − |

choriambic cadence: | − x x − |

paeonic cadence (first paeonic): | − x x x |

C. Feet

iamb: | x − |

trochee: | − x |

anapest: | x x − |

dactyl: | − x x |

ionic (double foot): | x x − − |

dipod (double foot): | ⸚ ⸚ |
| ⸚ ⸚ |
| ⸚ (p) |

trimeter: 3 feet

tetrameter: 4 feet

pentameter: 5 feet

hexameter: 6 feet

heptameter: 7 feet

heroic line: iambic pentameter

alexandrine: iambic hexameter

septenary: iambic heptameter

D. The Iambic Pentameter

form (matrix, norm line): | x − | x − | x − | x − | x − |

variations:

trochaic substitution | − x |

elision   ⌣

feminine ending   . . . x −| x

double feminine ending   . . . x −| x x

ionic substitution | x x − − |

truncation | − | x − | . . .

anacrusis   x|x − | . . .

alexandrine (iambic hexameter line)

amphibious section   ⌐‾‾‾⌐‾‾⌐   − ⌐‾‾ − ⌐‾‾⌐

modulations:

modification

    promotion

    demotion

alteration

    compression

    extension

E. Types of Cesura:

feminine: x ‖

masculine: − ‖

medial: after syll. 4, 5, 6.

lyric: | x ‖ − | (cesura divides normal foot)

epic: | x −| x‖ x − | (extra slack before cesura)

truncated: | x − ‖ − | x − |

anacrusis: | x − ‖ x x − | x − |

F. Stanzas

couplet   *aa bb cc*

triplet   *aaa bbb ccc*

tercet   *aba bcb cdc*

terza rima $^5aba\ bcb\ cdc$

heroic quatrain ^5abab

Rubaiyat Stanza ^5aaxa

In Memoriam Stanza ^4abba

cinquain   *2–4–6–8–2 syll.*

Venus and Adonis Stanza ^5ababcc

Romance Six, tail-rhyme stanza, rime couée $^4aa^3b^4aa^3b$
    or $^4aa^3b^4cc^3b$

Burns Stanza $^4aaa^2b^4a^2b$

rime royal $^5ababbcc$

Monk's Tale Stanza $^5ababbcbc$

ottava rima $^5abababcc$

triolet   *ABaAabAB*

Spenserian Stanza $^5ababbcbc^6c$

Italian sonnet $^5abba\ abba\ \left|\begin{array}{l}cdcdcd \\ cde\ \ cde\end{array}\right.$

English sonnet $^5abab\ cdcd\ efef\ gg$

rondeau   *aabba aab–R aabba–R*

rondel   *ABba abAB abbaAB*

Epithalamion Stanza $^5ababc^3c^5dcde^3e^5fggfh^3h^5r^6R$

villanelle   *A'bA" abA' abA" abA' abA" abA'A"*

ballade stanza   *ababbcbC*

sestina formula   *6 1 5 2 4 3*

G. Abbreviations

FM	Folk Meter
LM	Long Measure
CM	Common Measure
HM	Half Measure
SM	Short Measure
PM	Poulter's Measure
D	(after other abbreviation): doubled (before other abbreviation): dipodic
DCMD	dipodic Common Measure doubled
DFM	dipodic folk meter
S	stress
SV	stress-verse
SSV	syllable-stress verse; foot-verse
SyV	syllabic verse
12er	twelver
14er	fourteener
16er	sixteener
APM	accentual Poulter's Measure
SyPM	syllabic Poulter's Measure
IP	iambic pentameter
BV	blank verse
HV	heroic verse
HC	heroic couplets
FV	free verse

CFV	cadenced free verse
AFV	accentual free verse; primary-stress verse
4s, 5s . .	4-stress, 5-stress, etc.
abc . . .	(rhyme scheme)
x	unrhymed line
ABC . . .	repeated word or line

H. Symbols of Scansion

‒ .	stress
1 2 3 4 . . .	stresses
´	stress or secondary stress
˝	primary stress
x	slack
|	foot bar
‖	cesura
(p), p, ( )	pause, musical pause, compensatory pause
˄	medial syllable
≏	medial counted as stress (promoted)
x̂	medial counted as slack (demoted)
◡ , ⌒	elision
◡̌ , ⌃	hovering accent
#	end of count (of syllables, stresses, etc.). Strophe boundary in cadenced free verse.

INDEX